The Northwest Ordinance
1787
A Bicentennial Handbook

Contributors

Robert G. Barrows, editor, Indiana Historical Bureau, Indianapolis, Indiana

Andrew R. L. Cayton, assistant professor of history, Ball State University, Muncie, Indiana

Patrick J. Furlong, professor of history, Indiana University South Bend, South Bend, Indiana

George W. Geib, professor of history, Butler University, Indianapolis, Indiana

Peter T. Harstad, executive director, Indiana Historical Society, Indianapolis, Indiana

Willard Heiss, genealogist, Indianapolis, Indiana

Lloyd A. Hunter, professor of history, Franklin College, Franklin, Indiana

Alan F. January, historian, the Centennial History of the Indiana General Assembly, Indianapolis, Indiana

Henry C. Karlson, professor of law, Indiana University School of Law, Indianapolis, Indiana

Shirley A. McCord, editor, Indiana Historical Bureau, Indianapolis, Indiana

James H. Madison, associate professor of history, Indiana University, Bloomington, Indiana

John W. Miller, director, Newspaper Microfilming Project, Indiana Historical Society, Indianapolis, Indiana

Mark E. Neely, director, the Louis A. Warren Lincoln Library and Museum, Fort Wayne, Indiana

Bernard W. Sheehan, professor of history, Indiana University, Bloomington, Indiana

Raymond L. Shoemaker, assistant executive director and business manager, Indiana Historical Society, Indianapolis, Indiana

Rebecca S. Shoemaker, associate professor of history, Indiana State University, Terre Haute, Indiana

Robert M. Taylor, Jr., Indiana Historical Society, Indianapolis, Indiana

Emma Lou Thornbrough, professor emeritus, Butler University, Indianapolis, Indiana

David G. Vanderstel, senior historian, Conner Prairie Pioneer Settlement, Noblesville, Indiana

THE
NORTHWEST ORDINANCE
1787

A Bicentennial
Handbook

Edited by
Robert M. Taylor, Jr.

Indianapolis
Indiana Historical Society
1987

Cover: "Upper Territories of the
United States," Mathew Carey,
Philadelphia, 1814.

© 1987 Indiana Historical Society

Library of Congress Cataloging in Publication Data

The Northwest Ordinance, 1787.

   Includes annotated text of the ordinance.
   Bibliography: p.
   Includes index.
   1. United States. Ordinance of 1787.   2. Northwest,
Old—History—1775–1865.   I. Taylor, Robert M.,
1941– . II. United States. Ordinance of 1787.
1987.
E309.N67   1987   977'.02   87–3674
ISBN 0–87195–008–1

The following publishers have generously given permission to use maps or
illustrations from copyrighted works: From *President Washington's Indian War: The
Struggle for the Old Northwest, 1790–1795*, by Wiley Sword. Copyright 1985 by the
University of Oklahoma Press. From *Encyclopedia of American History*, updated
and revised, edited by Richard B. Morris, "United States after 1783" (map, p.
108). Copyright 1953, 1961, 1965 by Harper and Row, Publishers, Inc. Reprinted
by permission of Harper and Row, Publishers, Inc.

Contents

Illustrations

Following page 30

Maps

Following page 78

Foreword

THE NORTHWEST ORDINANCE OF 1787 is among the most important documents in American history. The bicentennial celebration of its origins provides an opportunity to think seriously about its fundamental place in the history of the nation and the history of Indiana.

The immediate purpose of the Ordinance was to create a government for the frontier lands that eventually came to be the states of Indiana, Ohio, Illinois, Michigan, and Wisconsin. To provide that government, however, the founding generation had to face some of the most difficult political questions of its time—questions that remain fundamental in our own time. The Northwest Ordinance addressed the challenges of representative government, the westward movement, federal-state relations, sectionalism and slavery, individual rights, and, ultimately, the nature of democracy. The Ordinance was inevitably a controversial document, but it was ultimately a successful document, particularly in binding the frontier to the new nation. Hoosiers, from the beginning, were Americans.

The essays and annotations of this publication provide an opportunity for citizens and students to consider thoughtfully not only the immediate history of the Northwest Ordinance but also basic and enduring issues in American political life. In recognizing that history is more than the bleached bones of dry fact, readers will join in appreciation of those responsible for this publication: the Indiana Historical Society, publisher of this bicentennial volume; the editor, Robert M. Taylor, Jr.; and the fine Indiana historians who have contributed the fruits of their scholarship.

James H. Madison
Indiana University, Bloomington

Introduction

ORDERLINESS WAS AN IDEAL of the era. Yet, as the year 1787 opened, chaos reigned in the back country north of the Ohio River. British soldiers manned military posts on the American side of the Great Lakes. Influential land speculators jockeyed for control of vast acreages in the Ohio country so that they could profit by selling farms and city lots to settlers. Indian leaders pledged death to frontiersmen bold enough to advance onto their lands. Settlers who contemplated that risk knew that there would be no government to "establish justice, insure domestic tranquility," or even to "provide for the common defence." Congress under the Articles of Confederation even failed to respond decisively to a report of Secretary of War Henry Knox that its army was "utterly incompetent" to secure the frontier. Meanwhile, men and forces were at work to supersede that Congress.

July 1787 brought a turning point in the affairs of the young republic, not because outstanding problems were solved, but because leaders agreed upon how to cope with them. On July 13 Congress, meeting in New York City, passed "An Ordinance for the Government of the Territory of the United States, North-west of the River Ohio." Before the month was out delegates to a federal convention in Philadelphia had hammered out the basic principles for a constitution with internal checks and balances. On September 17 they approved of the wording for that document which (after public discussion, ratification, and the addition of a Bill of Rights) Americans use to this day to govern themselves. Both documents resulted from the eighteenth-century quest for order in public affairs. Both proved to be durable as well as applicable to wider geographical areas than stipulated in their texts. Both addressed universals in a practical manner that Americans could accept.

The relationship between the Northwest Ordinance and the United States Constitution captivated no less a mind than that of Abraham Lincoln. The mature Lincoln coupled these two documents in a manner which bore directly upon his interpretation of the Union. He explained to an Indianapolis audience on September 19, 1859:

> The ordinance of 1787 was passed simultaneously with the making of the Constitution of the United States. It prohibited the taking of slavery into the North-western Territory. . . . There was nothing said in the Constitution relative to the spread of slavery in the Territories, but the same generation of men said something about it in this ordinance of '87, through the influence of which you of Indiana, and your neighbors in Ohio, Illinois, Wisconsin and Michigan, are prosperous, free men. . . . Our fathers who made the government, made the ordinance of 1787.

This argument he developed more fully and reasoned more closely at the Cooper Institute in New York City, February 27, 1860. The Congress under the new constitution clinched his point, he asserted, when it reaffirmed the Northwest Ordinance in 1789. The intent of the founding fathers was clear—the central government was supreme and could impose conditions upon the territories and states. Lincoln's interpretation of the two basic documents of 1787 helped him steer the Union through its greatest crisis and gave his nationalism the flavor of the Old Northwest.

But that is jumping ahead in the story. This book is designed to provide a framework for discussing and understanding the text of the Northwest Ordinance as well as the issues and meaning behind the text. Robert M. Taylor, Jr., coordinator of the Indiana Historical Society's efforts in recognition of the bicentennials of the Northwest Ordinance and the United States Constitution, approached Indiana scholars to prepare the commentary and the annotation that follow. He urged them to write for readers representing a range of ages and interests within and beyond the classrooms of the state and to refrain from addressing only their professional colleagues. During the editorial process both Taylor and Kent Calder of the Society's Publications Division took special care to clarify points for non specialists. However, the contributors were not expected to submit bland, "generic" copy nor to resolve all differences of interpretation they hold collectively. Nor did the editors strive to eliminate all "overlap." Readers should be aware of this at the outset, as well as the fact that some sections of the Ordinance invite more elucidation than others.

The book is divided into three main parts. The first provides a background to the Ordinance and its passage by the Confederation Congress. In the lead essay, Andrew Cayton discusses the Ordinance from the point of view of three groups of people living on the frontier—Indians, Anglo-Americans, and French—and the displacement of their social and cultural arrangements by the values and structures of American society to the east. The question arises—did those dwelling on the frontier comprise a society (or societies) however defined? Were the Anglo-American squatters nearer in frame of mind to their French co-residents of the frontier, to the Indians, or to the Americans who drafted documents of state in New York and Philadelphia?

In an accompanying essay Robert M. Taylor, Jr., introduces the relatively unknown men who voted on the Ordinance legislation in the Confederation Congress. He compares and contrasts their biographies with those of another group of men sitting in the Constitutional Convention in Philadelphia at the same time. He invites those inclined to cast aspersions on the Ordinance under the assumption that it was drafted by men decidedly inferior to those sitting in Philadelphia to reexamine their thinking.

The second part of the book comprises commentaries on specific sections and articles of the Ordinance itself. Young readers are forewarned that, in places, the Ordinance is difficult for all but trained lawyers to understand. (That is one reason why the Society decided upon this format for the book.) The second paragraph of the Ordinance, consisting of two long sentences setting forth rules of inheritance, is a case in point.

Those who continue on in the text of the Ordinance will come to other sections where great and timeless ideals are expressed in eloquent English rivaling that in the most quoted sections of the Declaration of Independence and the Constitution. The beginning sentence of Article Three, "Religion, Morality, and knowledge being necessary to good government and the happiness of mankind, Schools and the means of education shall forever be encouraged," is one candidate for that designation. What other sections may qualify? What of the pledge that the "utmost good faith shall always be observed towards the Indians"? Is it to be taken at face value, or was it an insincere use of pious phraseology? At several junctures critical readers will want to know how current strivings measure up to 1787 expectations.

While considering the text of the Northwest Ordinance and the commentary accompanying it, one might try to determine:

(1) which of its sections and principles emerged from the wellsprings of western civilization,

(2) which grew out of the British colonial experience in North America beginning at Jamestown in 1607,

(3) which addressed immediate problems of the late 1780s,

(4) which are primarily the products of original thought and planning, and

(5) which were genuine attempts to set a high tone for the young republic?

In the third part of the book Patrick Furlong discusses the transformation of a paper plan into a functioning government. He details the resulting problems and delays, the strife among officials, the divisions of the territory, and the quests for statehood. Three "Ps" serve as reader guideposts: personalities, process, and partisanship. Was French-speaking Arthur St. Clair a good choice for the governorship? Or was he an incorrigible foot-dragger, a poor soldier, and a worse politician? Could it be said that the three-stage process for the evolution of government was so superior that it could transform greed and other private vices into public virtues? What of the partisanship that had emerged by the time that the first state was created out of the Northwest Territory? Was it a curse or a boon to good government?

The volume also includes a chronology of events, a selected bibliography, and a series of maps, all of which bear directly upon the Northwest Ordinance and Northwest Territory.

The Indiana Historical Society expresses its appreciation to the scholars who have contributed to this volume and also to others who made valuable suggestions on content and format. The book is offered to the public to further understanding of an important American state paper of particular significance to the people of Indiana and the Old Northwest. If its pages serve as reminders of the value of forethought in public affairs, the energy used to produce them will not have been spent in vain.

Peter T. Harstad

Chronology

JULY 4, 1776: Continental Congress adopts the Declaration of Independence.

NOVEMBER 15, 1777: Congress passes Articles of Confederation.

MAY 15, 1778: George Rogers Clark captures Cahokia, near present St. Louis, thus commencing a campaign to wrest the the western lands from the British.

JULY 20, 1778: Clark captures Vincennes, a British post located on the Wabash River.

DECEMBER 9, 1778: Virginia annexes the territory won by Clark and calls it the County of Illinois.

SEPTEMBER 6, 1780: Congress recommends that states surrender "a portion of their territorial claims, since they cannot be preserved entire without endangering the stability of the general confederacy."

OCTOBER 10, 1780: Congress adopts a report on the disposition of ceded western territory which provides for the creation of distinct states of not less than 100 or more than 150 miles square. It also declares that states so formed "shall become members of the federal union, and have the same rights of sovereignty, freedom and independence, as the other states."

MARCH 1, 1781: Maryland ratifies the Articles of Confederation, which are then declared in force.

OCTOBER 29, 1782: Congress adopts a motion to accept New York's cession of its land in the western territory.

NOVEMBER 30, 1782: The United States signs a preliminary treaty with Great Britain that provides for the British to move from their fortifications in the Northwest and establishes the Mississippi River as the western boundary of the United States. The northern boundary between the United States and British Upper Canada (Ontario) is also established.

JUNE, 1783: The Newburgh Petition to Congress, drawn up by Rufus Putnam, asks on behalf of 288 Revolutionary officers that Indian lands northwest of the Ohio River be procured, surveyed, and given to the soldiers for services rendered.

SEPTEMBER 3, 1783: The Treaty of Paris is signed in France by the United States and Great Britain. With the treaty, Britain officially cedes its empire north of Florida and west of the Appalachian Mountains to the United States.

JANUARY 14, 1784: Congress ratifies the Treaty of Paris.

MARCH 1, 1784: Congress accepts Virginia's cession of its western land claims, which Virginia's general assembly had passed on October 20, 1783. The committee of the Confederation Congress, chaired by Thomas Jefferson, submits its proposal for temporary government in the Northwest Territory.

APRIL 23, 1784: Congress enacts Resolutions for the Government of the Western Territory (Ordinance of 1784). Though never really in force, the ordinance stood as the fundamental law for the western lands until repealed by the last clause of the Northwest Ordinance of 1787.

OCTOBER 22, 1784: By the Treaty of Fort Stanwix II in New York, the Iroquoian Six Nations surrender all claims to lands northwest of the Ohio River.

JANUARY 11, 1785: Congress moves to newly designated temporary capital, New York City, meeting in the City Hall until the permanent seat of government on the banks of the Delaware is ready.

JANUARY 21, 1785: By the Treaty of Fort McIntosh, Wyandot, Chippewa, Delaware, and Ottawa nations cede land in the Ohio country.

MARCH 28, 1785: Mount Vernon Conference of commissioners from Maryland and Virginia convenes to discuss local navigation problems.

APRIL 19, 1785: Congress accepts Massachusetts's cession of its western land claims, which amounts to 54,000 square miles.

MAY 20, 1785: The Land Ordinance of 1785 passes Congress. It provides for the survey and sale of western lands and lays the foundation of American land policy until the passage of the Homestead Act in 1862.

JANUARY 21, 1786: Virginia's legislature invites all the states to a September meeting in Annapolis to discuss commercial problems.

FEBRUARY 1, 1786: Shawnee Indians sign the Treaty of Fort Finney, relinquishing tribal land claims east of the Great Miami.

FEBRUARY 28, 1786: British refuse to abandon their military posts along the American northwestern frontier. These include forts at Oswego, New York, at Detroit, and at Michilimackinac, at the entrance to Lake Michigan.

MARCH 1, 1786: The Ohio Company of Associates is founded at the Bunch of Grapes tavern in Boston, Massachusetts, by Rufus Putnam, Benjamin Tupper, and Manasseh Cutler for the purpose of buying and settling federal lands northwest of the Ohio River.

MAY 10, 1786: A congressional committee led by James Monroe formulates the fundamental principles for the administrative organization of the territory northwest of the Ohio River.

MAY 26, 1786: Congress accepts Connecticut's cession of its lands, except for the Western Reserve, in the Northwest Territory.

SEPTEMBER 11–14, 1786: Five states send a total of twelve delegates to the Annapolis Convention. The convention adopts a resolution on September 14, drafted by Alexander Hamilton, asking all states to send representatives to a new convention to be held in Philadelphia in May of 1787 to discuss commercial issues and also "to render the constitution of the Federal Government adequate to the exigencies of the Union."

SEPTEMBER 18, 1786: Congress appoints a new committee to report on a temporary government for the western territory. One of its members is Nathan Dane.

FEBRUARY 21, 1787: Congress adopts a resolution calling for a Constitutional Convention to assemble on May 14, 1787.

APRIL 23, 1787: A congressional committee reports an "Ordinance for the Government of the Western Territory." The third reading of the bill takes place on May 10, but action on the legislation is postponed.

MAY 9, 1787: Gen. Samuel H. Parsons, on behalf of the Ohio Company of Associates, places before Congress a memorial asking that "a Tract of Country within the Western Territory of the United States at some convenient Place may be granted them at a reasonable price."

MAY 25, 1787: Constitutional Convention opens in Philadelphia.

JULY 9, 1787: The "Ordinance for the government of the Western Territory" is referred to a new committee made up of Edward Carrington, Richard Henry Lee, Nathan Dane, Melancthon Smith, and John Kean.

JULY 13, 1787: Congress passes "An Ordinance for the Government of the Territory North-west of the River Ohio."

SEPTEMBER 17, 1787: The United States Constitution is approved, and a letter of transmittal to Congress is drafted. The Constitutional Convention formally adjourns.

SEPTEMBER 28, 1787: Congress resolves to submit the Constitution to the states for ratification.

OCTOBER 5, 1787: Arthur St. Clair is appointed governor of the Northwest Territory.

OCTOBER 27, 1787: The Ohio Company of Associates contracts with the Federal Government for the purchase of 1.5 million acres of land in the Ohio country on the Muskingum River, with an option on another 5 million acres assigned to the Scioto Company.

APRIL 7, 1788: Marietta is founded by a group of pioneers of the Ohio Company of Associates. It is the first legal settlement in the Northwest Territory.

JUNE 21, 1788: The Constitution is ratified and becomes effective when New Hampshire becomes the ninth state to approve it.

JULY 15, 1788: Gov. Arthur St. Clair arrives at Marietta to inaugurate civil government in the territory.

JULY 27, 1788: The Scioto Company purchases 4,901,480 acres in the Ohio country to the north of the land owned by the Ohio Company of Associates. Governor St. Clair organizes Washington County, which covers about one-half of present Ohio.

AUGUST 17, 1788: The town of Losantiville (later Cincinnati) is founded.

OCTOBER 10, 1788: The old Confederation Congress conducts its last official business.

OCTOBER 15, 1788: Final contract made between Congress and John Cleves Symmes for the Symmes Purchase, or the Miami

Purchase, for one million acres. The land was subsequently surveyed at 311,682 acres.

JANUARY 9, 1789: Treaty of Fort Harmar, in the Ohio country, confirms western boundaries established in treaties of Fort Stanwix (1784) and Fort McIntosh (1785).

MARCH 4, 1789: The first Federal Congress convenes in New York City.

APRIL 30, 1789: George Washington is inaugurated as the nation's first president under the Constitution.

AUGUST 7, 1789: Congress passes an act making minor changes in the Ordinance of 1787 to bring it into conformity with the Constitution.

SEPTEMBER 25, 1789: Congress submits to the states twelve amendments, ten of which form the Bill of Rights.

MAY 26, 1790: The "Territory South of the River Ohio" is officially established. This territory was the state of Franklin from 1785 to 1788, unrecognized by either North Carolina or by Congress.

DECEMBER 15, 1791: Virginia ratifies the Bill of Rights, making it part of the United States Constitution.

AUGUST 20, 1794: Gen. Anthony Wayne defeats a large Indian army at the Battle of Fallen Timbers in the northwestern Ohio country.

NOVEMBER 19, 1794: Jay's Treaty between Great Britain and the United States requires British withdrawal from their Northwest posts on or before June 1, 1796. President Washington signs the treaty August 3, 1795.

MAY 29, 1795: Governor St. Clair and the territorial judges convene at Cincinnati and adopt an elaborate set of laws derived from the various states. These laws have been called Maxwell's Code because Maxwell was the name of the local printer.

JULY 19, 1795: The Connecticut Land Company purchases a large tract on Lake Erie in the northeastern Ohio country. Moses Cleaveland is the company agent.

AUGUST 3, 1795: The Treaty of Greenville is signed by Gen. Anthony Wayne and twelve Ohio and Great Lakes tribes. The treaty makes white settlement possible in two-thirds of the present state of Ohio and sends Ohio's Indians onto reservations.

OCTOBER 27, 1795: The Treaty of San Lorenzo (Pinckney's Treaty) with Spain establishes southern and western borders and gives Americans free navigation of the Mississippi and the right to deposit cargo at the New Orleans port.

MAY 18, 1796: Congress passes the Land Act of 1796, providing for surveys of all public lands within the Northwest Territory, public auctions of the lands, and the setting up of land offices in Cincinnati and Pittsburgh. The minimum sale of 640 acres at $2.00 per acre, payable in one year, benefited large-scale land speculators.

OCTOBER 12, 1798: Mississippi Territory organized with its capital at Natchez.

SEPTEMBER 24, 1799: With a population of 5,000 free adult males, the first legislature of the Northwest Territory convenes at Chillicothe, thus launching the second stage of territorial government.

OCTOBER 3, 1799: William Henry Harrison is chosen by the territorial assembly to be its congressional delegate.

MARCH 20, 1800: A bill is introduced in the House of Representatives for dividing of the Northwest Territory into two separate governments.

MAY 7, 1800: President Adams approves the division of the Northwest Territory, creating the Indiana Territory, after a congressional conference committee reaches an accord on the provisions.

MAY 10, 1800: Congress passes the Land Act of 1800 (Harrison Act), liberalizing credit terms and lowering minimum acreage for purchasing public lands.

MAY 13, 1800: President Adams appoints William Henry Harrison the first governor of the Indiana Territory.

JANUARY 7, 1802: Western University, the first in the Northwest Territory, is chartered at the village of Athens. The school is renamed Ohio University in 1804.

APRIL 30, 1802: A congressional enabling act receives executive approval for the creation of a new state from the eastern division of the Northwest Territory.

NOVEMBER 1–26, 1802: Northwest Territory (Ohio) delegates convene in Chillicothe to prepare application for statehood.

MARCH 1, 1803: Ohio becomes the seventeenth state, the first to be created from the Northwest Territory.

APRIL 30–MAY 2, 1803: France cedes all of Louisiana to the United States, doubling the size of the nation.

MARCH 26, 1804: The Louisiana Purchase area is divided into the Territory of Orleans and the District of Louisiana, with the latter supervised by the officials of the Indiana Territory. In 1812 Orleans Territory becomes the State of Louisiana, and the District of Louisiana becomes Missouri Territory.

MARCH 26, 1804: The Land Act of 1804 authorizes sale of quarter sections and reduces minimum payment per acre to $1.64.

DECEMBER 5, 1804: Governor Harrison declares that Indiana Territory has passed into the second, or representative, stage of government, and he calls for the election of nine representatives for a lower house of the legislative assembly.

JANUARY 11, 1805: Congress detaches Wayne County from Indiana Territory and creates Michigan Territory, with Detroit as the capital and William Hull as the governor.

JULY 29, 1805: The first session of the Indiana Territory's general assembly gets underway.

FEBRUARY 3, 1809: Congress carves the Illinois Territory from the Indiana Territory. The new terrritory is two and one-half times that of the present state. The first governor is Ninian Edwards.

JULY 2, 1809: Tecumseh, chief of the Shawnee tribe, and his brother, the Prophet, begin a campaign to organize an Indian Confederacy to fight incursions on their lands by white settlers north of the Ohio River.

NOVEMBER 6–8, 1811: The Battle of Tippecanoe in the Indiana Territory shatters the Indian confederacy.

NOVEMBER 20, 1811: Construction of the National Road begins in Cumberland, Maryland. By 1840 the road reaches its termination in Illinois.

DECEMBER 11, 1811: The Indiana Territory House of Representatives adopts a memorial to Congress asking permission for the citizens of Indiana Territory to write a state constitution and be admitted to the Union.

JUNE 18, 1812: Congress declares war on Great Britain.

DECEMBER 28, 1812: William Henry Harrison resigns as governor of the Indiana Territory and is replaced by John Gibson. In January 1813 Harrison is given command of all United States land forces in the West.

FEBRUARY 20, 1813: President Madison appoints Lewis Cass governor of the Michigan Territory.

MARCH 3, 1813: President Madison appoints Thomas Posey, a Virginian, the new governor of the Indiana Territory.

MAY 1, 1813: Corydon becomes the new capital of the Indiana Territory.

DECEMBER 24, 1814: Treaty of Ghent signed, ending the War of 1812. The treaty is ratified on February 16, 1815.

JANUARY 1, 1816: The newly laid-out town of Columbus replaces Chillicothe as the capital of Ohio.

APRIL 19, 1816: President Madison approves an enabling act which authorizes the formation of a constitution and a state government for Indiana.

JUNE 10, 1816: The Indiana Constitutional Convention convenes at Corydon.

JUNE 29, 1816: The constitutional convention finishes its work.

DECEMBER 11, 1816: President Madison approves a resolution admitting Indiana as the nineteenth state.

APRIL 18, 1818: Congress passes an enabling act to make Illinois a state.

DECEMBER 3, 1818: Illinois becomes the nation's twenty-first state, with its capital at Kaskaskia. The northern part of Illinois Territory is added to Michigan Territory.

JANUARY 25, 1820: The state capital of Illinois is moved from Kaskaskia to Vandalia.

APRIL 24, 1820: A Land Act abolishes credit for land purchases from public domain but reduces the minimum price per acre to $1.25.

JANUARY, 1825: Indiana's capital is moved from Corydon to Indianapolis.

MAY 11–JUNE 29, 1835: A constitution is developed for Michigan by a convention meeting in Detroit.

APRIL 20, 1836: The Wisconsin Territory is formed, comprising all of Michigan Territory from the Great Lakes west to the Missouri, north of the states of Illinois and Missouri. Henry Dodge is the first governor.

JANUARY 22, 1837: Michigan comes into the Union as its twenty-sixth state. The Upper Peninsula of Wisconsin Territory is added to Michigan, and Detroit is the first state capital. The capital is moved to Lansing in 1850.

JUNE 12, 1838: The western part of Wisconsin Territory between the Mississippi and Missouri rivers is organized as the Iowa Territory, with Iowa City as its capital.

MAY 29, 1848: Wisconsin comes into the Union as the thirtieth state.

MAY 3, 1849: Minnesota Territory is organized, with Alexander Ramsey as governor and St. Paul as the capital.

OCTOBER 13, 1857: Residents of Minnesota Territory vote to adopt a constitution and apply for statehood.

MAY 11, 1858: Eastern Minnesota Territory becomes the thirty-second state. The western part remains Minnesota Territory, which on March 2, 1861, becomes part of the Dakota Territory.

The Northwest Ordinance from the Perspective of the Frontier

BY

ANDREW R. L. CAYTON

 THE EVENTS OF THE YEAR 1787 were among the most dramatic and most decisive in the history of the United States. In January, an army raised by the Commonwealth of Massachusetts suppressed Shays's Rebellion, an uprising of farmers provoked by high taxes and an unresponsive legislature. In May, amid rumors of disunion and fears of anarchy fueled by the armed insurrection in Massachusetts, delegates from twelve states began meeting behind closed doors in Philadelphia in an effort to revise and to strengthen the system of national government maintained under the Articles of Confederation. In September, the Philadelphia convention presented the results of its summer-long deliberations to the public in a proposed new national constitution. Meanwhile, members of Congress, not content to be mere spectators in a year of such great significance, passed an ordinance for the government of the Northwest Territory on July 13. They intended this act to be the blueprint for the expansion of the American republic.

These three events were more than superficially related. The men who put down Shays's Rebellion and those who wrote the Constitution and the Northwest Ordinance shared the same ideological perspective. In a very real

[1]

sense, the suppression of Shays's Rebellion and the writing of the Constitution and the Northwest Ordinance were official announcements of the new order created by the American Revolution. Each defined the United States as a republic governed by the authority of popularly elected institutions which would act as checks or filters on the will of the people. Implicit in the events of 1787 was a vision of a nation dedicated to enlightened principles of reason, genteel manners, and complex economic development. The United States would be a nation that looked to the future as a stable and prosperous empire—the embodiment of the highest levels of social and economic development, the very model of a progressive and interdependent society.[1] As powerful as this vision was, however, it was one that was very much at odds with the characters and interests of many Americans.

Historians have told us much about popular support for the Shaysites and opposition to the Constitution. But we know much less about contemporary reaction to the Northwest Ordinance. Some of the reasons for this gap in our knowledge—such as the fact that the American people never debated the Ordinance publicly and the relative lack of sources about life north of the Ohio River before 1787—are obvious. But others follow from the assumptions and methodology that most scholars have brought to the study of the subject. By and large they have examined the Ordinance from a political or constitutional perspective. This approach has produced a sophisticated understanding of how and why Congress passed the act that it did. We know that the Ordinance was neither a rejection of the Ordinance of 1784 nor an effort to appease the demands of speculative land companies. We see the legislation of July 1787 as the climax of a long discussion among America's leaders about how the new republic should handle both the establishment of colonies and their ultimate acceptance into the Union on an equal basis with the thirteen original states.[2]

To look at American territorial policy in the 1780s

solely from the perspective of Congress, however, is to limit our understanding of that policy. Most critically, this perspective reinforces the assumption of many contemporaries that the land north of the Ohio River was "virgin land"—a region to be settled and developed in the image of the new American order. Many government officials shared the belief of the Rev. Manasseh Cutler, one of the leading members of the Ohio Company of Associates which founded the first permanent settlement in the Northwest Territory, that on the frontier there "will be no wrong habits to combat, and no inveterate systems to overturn—there is no rubbish to remove, before you can lay the foundation."[3]

In fact, of course, the Northwest Territory in the 1780s was the home of thousands of men and women. From the perspectives of Indians; French settlers at Vincennes, Kaskaskia, and Cahokia; and Anglo-American frontiersmen, the territorial policy of the Congress of the United States posed a severe threat to their ways of life. The Ordinance of July 1787 was more a blueprint of political and social conquest than a blueprint for the peaceful expansion of a stable republican empire. Viewing the Ordinance from the perspective of the frontier can help us to understand more fully the implications and consequences of the vision of the American future contained in the suppression of Shays's Rebellion and the promulgation of the Constitution of the United States. It removes the discussion from the realm of congressional debates and places it in the context of its impact on the lives and society of the people whom it most directly and immediately affected. In the end, the key point that this perspective suggests is that by helping to define and legitimize the new order of post-revolutionary America the Northwest Ordinance helped to define alternative social and political conceptions as anachronistic, barbaric, or anarchic, and therefore illegitimate.

In the 1780s, the Northwest Territory was a classic example of a frontier in the sense that no group of people exercised unchallenged power over it.[4] The locus of sovereignty, meaning the right to govern, was very much in dispute. Indians, encouraged by the British from their headquarters at Detroit, and various groups of Americans claimed the region as their own. The most practical problem facing members of the American Congress, then, was to establish their authority as the only legitimate source of power north of the Ohio River. The task involved more than gaining territorial and political dominance; it also required Congress to control the social and economic structures of the region.

The human obstacles to congressional power were diverse and powerful. Foremost among them were the Indian tribes—specifically, the Delawares, the Shawnee, and the Miamis—who occupied much of what is now Ohio and Indiana. These Indians had not lived in the region for very long; under pressure from white population growth and the powerful Iroquois confederacy, they had migrated west from eastern Pennsylvania in the middle of the eighteenth century. But the westward expansion of Anglo-Americans quickly caught up with them. From the 1760s through the 1790s most of the Indians in the Ohio Valley were involved in sporadic but intense warfare with white settlers in Pennsylvania and western Virginia. Much of the time the Indians acted with the aid and encouragement of British officials at Detroit.[5]

After the American Revolution, the government of the United States moved to negotiate with the Indians for possession of the Ohio Country. American commissioners met with representatives of the Delawares, Wyandots, Chippewas, and Ottawas at Fort McIntosh in January 1785 and with the Shawnee at Fort Finney in January 1786. The United States government insisted upon dealing with the Indians as the defeated allies of the British. According to Congress, the treaties of forts McIntosh and Finney were the counterparts of the Treaty of Paris signed with the British in 1783. Perplexed by the American assertion of their defeated status and confused

about the position of the British, the Indian representatives agreed to surrender their claims to the lands
east of the Miami River and to recognize the sovereignty
of the United States over their villages. But many Delawares and Shawnee refused to accept the legitimacy of
the treaties. Raids and counterraids continued to be an
irregular but deadly part of life in the Ohio Valley in the
1780s. By 1787, in fact, the United States government
had made no real progress toward a mutually acceptable
agreement with the Indians who resided in the Northwest
Territory.[6]

Congress, however, had acquired undisputed authority over the region within the American political structure.
The national government claimed the right to control the
Northwest Territory by virtue of various states' cessions of
their claims. The most important of these cessions was that
of Virginia in 1784. The intention of Congress was to survey and sell the lands north of the Ohio River in order to
retire the national debt and to provide the national government, which lacked the power to tax under the Articles of
Confederation, with a steady source of income.[7]

Unfortunately for Congress, many individual Americans in the 1780s continued to dispute the authority of any
eastern government over the lands north of the Ohio. Such
people included residents of Pennsylvania and Virginia
who were settling illegally, or squatting, to use the pejora-
tive term, along the northern bank of the Ohio and in the
valleys of its tributaries. These "intruders," as congressmen
labeled them, were looking for better land and more plen-
tiful hunting. In a larger sense, their migration across the
Ohio was nothing more than a continuation of the gener-
ational waves of Anglo-American expansion. There was
one legal settlement of Americans north of the Ohio River.
Across from Louisville, families had settled on 150,000
acres granted by Virginia to participants in the military
expeditions of George Rogers Clark during the American
Revolution. American hunters and trappers also regularly
moved through the forests of the Northwest Territory. By

and large these people had little respect for either the authority or wishes of Congress. They defied proclamations, laws, and treaties to such an extent that government troops stationed in the Ohio Valley in the 1780s devoted much of their time to evicting squatters and attempting to control other frontiersmen. Indeed, government officials by 1787 had long since realized that peace and stability in the Northwest Territory depended on their ability to make whites as well as Indians respect the supreme authority of Congress.[8]

The most established residents of the Northwest Territory in the 1780s were the largely French residents of villages established in the early eighteenth century at Vincennes, Kaskaskia, and Cahokia. Numbering only in the hundreds, these settlers nonetheless were people whose values and customs were markedly different from those of Americans living along the Atlantic seaboard. They, too, would have to accept the sovereignty of Congress if the American government was going to exercise complete power in the Northwest.[9]

The Indians, Anglo-Americans, and French living in or near the Northwest Territory in the late eighteenth century were obviously not the best of friends. To the contrary, they often dealt with each other through brutal torture and murder. Each community had its own language and customs, and yet these three groups had a great deal more in common with each other than might appear at first glance. The Delawares and the Shawnee had been living in close proximity to whites for a century; they had become heavily dependent on trade with Europeans for supplies and implements (such as whiskey and rifles) that they were technologically incapable of producing themselves. Whites, on the other hand, had assimilated valuable pieces of Indian culture into their society.[10] Although they were very often bitter enemies, whites and Indians in the Ohio Valley shared many cultural characteristics.

Certainly in the eyes of the men who devised American territorial policy in the 1780s Indians, white frontiersmen, and French settlers seemed to share similar traits. In particular, they behaved in ways that government officials and their friends believed were antithetical to the goals of a republican government that were implicit in the Constitution and the Northwest Ordinance. Congressmen, surveyors, army officers, and settlers from the East who arrived after 1787 frequently used the same adjectives to describe both the Native- and the Anglo-Americans residing in the Northwest Territory. They were, variously, lazy, barbaric, ignorant, uncivilized, disrespectful of all legal authority, and anarchic; they lacked ambition and interest in improving their society. All lived what was often called a primitive, or Indian, style of life. Connecticut-born Samuel Holden Parsons, one of the first judges of the Northwest Territory, referred to white frontiersmen he encountered as "our own white savages."[11]

So, too, territorial officials described the French settlers in the Illinois country as lazy and ignorant. Easterners were simply astonished that any peoples, white or red, would live in the dirty and backward conditions they found on the frontier. In short, their conceptions of Indians and white frontiersmen were the opposite of their image of the ideal citizen of a republic.[12]

Most well-educated Americans, including those who wrote the Constitution and the Northwest Ordinance, assumed that all societies passed through predictable stages of social and economic development. The history of the western world, they believed, was a cycle of individual progressions from barbarism to civilization followed sadly but inevitably by rapid declines back to the depths of barbarism as people became selfish and indolent. The tragic histories of Greece and Rome exemplified this pattern. In the first stages, men and women lived in isolation. Their lives were geared to subsistence economies; they had little interest in education or refinement. On the other extreme, in societies at the highest level of development, people lived in a world of interdependence. International commerce and economic specialization marked their lives; they devoted increasing amounts of time to polishing and ornamenting themselves and their world. In the former kind of society, people dealt with each other in the most primitive ways imaginable: local prejudices stood in the way of social harmony and fomented conflict and contention. In the latter world, the peaceful exchange of both goods and ideas and the existence of powerful institutions, such as schools, churches, and governments, paved the way to harmony, balance, and order.[13] Given these assumptions and the expectations about the American future that follow from them, it is not surprising that the government officials and educated easterners who held them condemned both whites and Indians for their primitive lifestyles.

In general, members of Congress in 1787 were attempting to fashion a colonial policy for a nation committed to the world of international commerce capitalism. Most of them were products of the most economically dynamic parts of the new country, the cities and major river valleys of the eastern seaboard. There, entrepreneurially minded individuals were involved in patterns of trade which extended from the Chesapeake Bay to London and Lisbon, from Philadelphia and New York to the Gold Coast of Africa, and from Boston to the ports of Chile and China. They exchanged the largely agricultural products of America for finished goods and exotic spices. During the wars of the French Revolution (1793–1815), the growing demand for cotton and foodstuffs fueled a rapid and virtually unprecedented expansion and diversification of the American economy.[14]

Men heavily involved in this worldwide trade tended to embrace a distinctive ideology in response to the structures of their material lives. The importance of free trade, the sanctity of private property over community notions of public property, and the belief that the supply and demand of the marketplace was the most effective arbitrator of human conflicts and social needs all came easily to them. These somewhat novel ideas (in the late eighteenth century) helped them to make sense of the complex, specialized, and far-flung economic world in which they operated. Merchants, artisans, and planters also found it imperative to put an end to the barriers that localism and ignorance often put in the way of international trade.

They also tended to adopt a revolutionary set of notions about individual behavior and social organization. While still far from the bourgeoisie of Victorian America, eighteenth-century entrepreneurs nonetheless began to preach the values of hard work, delayed gratification, and regular attention to one's business. In so doing, they explicitly attacked the mores of more traditional, locally oriented economies that centered on the household and the needs of families. In most of America, as in Europe, work followed the rhythms of the natural world, not the chimes of the countinghouse clock; men and women's work was intimately integrated into the rest of their lives. To speak of a place of business, of specialization, or of a segregation of work and play was to speak a language with which many people in eighteenth-century America were unfamiliar.[15]

For all these reasons, many men heavily involved in commerce in the most developed parts of the United States were strong supporters of the Constitution of the United States and the suppression of Shays's Rebellion. The quashing of the uprising in Massachusetts was a smashing of a dangerous spirit of localism and resistance to legal forms of government. The Constitution, on the other hand, created the skeleton of a great commercial empire—a nation unencumbered by parochial jealousies and state rivalries, a nation governed by laws and the requirements of the international marketplace of goods and ideas.

The embodiment of such notions with regard to the West was the Ohio Company of Associates, a joint-stock company of New England veterans of the American Revolution formed in 1786 to promote land speculation and settlement in the West. Manasseh Cutler, one of the five directors of the Ohio Company, was negotiating the purchase of one and one-half million acres of land from Congress at the same time the Northwest Ordinance was being written. Cutler's alliance with the speculator and entrepreneur William Duer and his participation in the Scioto Company, a huge enterprise that involved selling land in the Northwest Territory to Frenchmen, have produced a great deal of scholarly speculation about the motives of the Ohio Company and the congressmen who authored the Ordinance. There was a connection between the two, but it was almost exclusively in the realms of politics and ideology. The Ohio Company, which would lead the official settlement of the Old Northwest under congressional authority with the founding of a city at the confluence of the Muskingum and Ohio rivers called Marietta in April 1788, envisioned the creation of the heart of the American empire in the Ohio Valley. They expected to bring international trade, social stability, and the refinements of culture to the West. The associates hoped that their settlements would become the models for the future development of the American empire.[16]

Most of the people who were actually residing on the frontier in the 1780s did not share these ideas, not because they were ignorant or contrary, but because they did not share the same economic and social structures. They embraced a different set of beliefs and customs which explained the demands and problems of life in the Ohio Valley far better than the ideas of congressmen and land companies.

The dominant economic activity on the frontier in the 1780s was hunting. Most men fed their families with the meat of wild animals they tracked and killed. And frontier trade, while primitive by Eastern standards, revolved to a great extent around skins and furs. The Delawares and Shawnee had long traded animal hides and pelts for instruments and goods; so too, white frontiersmen bartered skins and fresh meat for supplies and goods they could not provide for themselves. Corn and other vegetables grown in small fields around cabins and the meat of pigs and cows supplemented frontier trade and diets. But the central occupation was that of hunter.[17]

The fact that survival depended to a great extent upon the availability and capture of wild animals meant that the demands of hunting had a tremendous impact on life in the Ohio Valley. These demands created, for example, a sexual division of labor that was unfamiliar to people in the East. During the American Revolution women had, at least briefly, assumed many (traditionally) male responsibilities while men were off at war. But on the frontier women did so regularly. Since men were gone on hunting and trapping expeditions for long periods of time, women in both Indian and white societies generally tended crops and handled the upkeep of home and farm. Eastern travelers and government officials frequently expressed dismay at finding women working in the fields while the men were off in the woods. But the men were not lazy, nor were they deserting or oppressing their women. The economic demands of the frontier simply mandated that men be gone much of the time.[18]

In the more complex economies of eastern America, moreover, hunting had moved to the periphery of social activities. Men's work was more specialized; artisans and professionals depended on an exchange of each other's services. Men with families rarely went off to work for more than a day. Their work habits, also, were fairly regular because they were tied to the demands of the markets in which they operated. Such men had come to look upon hunting and fishing as leisure activities, available only to men of wealth or to be indulged when taking time off from work. Frontiersmen and Indians thus naturally appeared to Eastern observers to be indolent, even presumptuous, in their pursuit of game. In the Ohio Valley, of course, hunting was the focus of the local economy, not an idle pleasure. But how one evaluated it depended entirely on one's perspective.

Hunting also underlay frontier attitudes toward land use, development, and social customs. In an economy geared to taking advantage of what the natural world had to offer, there was little incentive to tear down woods or to

put up fences. To the contrary, it offered every encouragement to leave the natural world alone. Improving land
by erecting elaborate towns or buildings would threaten
the very basis of the economy. Clearly, Indians and white
frontiersmen lived in what we would call primitive conditions. But to have planted large fields or cleared timber
or built roads and cities would have been to reform the
environment on which life depended. These people, for
better or worse, lived in a kind of symbiosis, albeit a
sometimes violent one, with the natural world; to improve
it, to develop it, to civilize it, to regularize it, was to de-
stroy it.

Similarly, the notion of private property, so critical in a
complex, interdependent market economy, was less important in a society of hunters. Which is not to say that
white frontiersmen and Indians did not care about protec-
ting their homes and fields. They surely did. Nonetheless,
there was a pronounced tendency to be more relaxed or
more careless about property rights.

The French, for example, according to Territorial Secretary Winthrop Sargent, kept over 5,000 acres in common.[19] The residents of Vincennes explained their failure to
divide their lands in a 1787 petition to Congress. Having
been "chiefly addicted to the Indian trade," they had "in a
great measure, overlooked the advantages that can be derived from the cultivation of lands. . . . Contented to raise
bread for our families, we neither extended our culture for
the purpose of exportation, nor formed an idea of dividing
among ourselves our fruitful country." But "the moment
we were connected with the United States, we began to be
sensible of the real value of lands."[20]

Many settlers from Kentucky who occupied land in
the Illinois country placed the blame for their inability to
develop their lands on the "hostile dispositions" of the
Indians. But whatever the cause, the results were the same.
These settlers reported to Congress in August 1787 that
they had been unable to begin agricultural cultivation or to
"define properly the lands which we meant to occupy."

Because they had been "penned up in forts & small garrisons," they had had to grow their crops in "a few fields tilled in common."[21]

Indians such as the Iroquois, meanwhile, viewed "all land" as "national land." According to Anthony F. C. Wallace, an individual could use a plot of land for private reasons, but when he abandoned the acreage it "reverted" to the community. There was, as Wallace observes, so much land that there was little incentive "to bother about individual ownership of real estate anyway." True, "economic security for both men and women lay in a proper recognition of one's obligation to family, clan, community, and nation, and in efficient and cooperative performances in team activities."[22]

Eastern observers and government officials often complained bitterly about lax land records, if they existed at all, and the absence of precise surveys and land boundaries. Sargent noted in August 1788 that land records at Vincennes were a mess. "There is scarcely one Case in twenty where the Title is complete—owing to the desultory Manner in which public Business has been transacted, & some other unfortunate Causes," he wrote.[23]

Once the government created by the Northwest Ordinance was in place, its officers moved to correct much of what they perceived to be irregularity in property matters. They adopted strict penalties for people who set fire to leaves and undergrowth in the woods, "thereby producing a conflagration prejudicial to the soil (and) destructive to the timber and improvements in the territory," even though such fires were regularly employed by Indians and white hunters to make the woods passable for both men and animals and to allow for unobstructed growth of vegetation. Territorial officials required the branding of all horses and cattle with a legally registered mark of ownership. They also laid down strict provisions for the erection of fences to protect farmers from stray animals; if an animal broke through a legal fence, the owner of the branded offender was responsible for all damages.[24] All of these acts in one way or another announced a new economic and social order on the frontier—one committed to the supremacy of the law and the protection of private property. But these regulations had little utility in a world of hunters and fur traders.

Neither did public education. Of what value was literacy in a world with few records, where the premium was on knowledge of animals and their environment that was acquired through experience? The frontier above all was an oral culture—a place where men and women told each other what they needed to know. The ability to read, while useful in certain situations, paled in significance when contrasted with the ability to spin a tale around a campfire or to explain the movements of deer. This was a world where men and women, often divided sexually for long periods of time because of the nature of their work, depended on interaction with family and friends for information and entertainment. It was a world, too, where men and women relaxed with the same intensity and in the same style with which they worked. Drinking, swearing, gambling, and swapping stories flavored leisure time, which, by the way, was often seasonal and did not conform to strict notions of regular, daily work.[25]

Governments beyond the local community were also generally perceived as greater sources of trouble than help. Certainly the Delaware and Shawnee Indians had every reason not to trust the orders and representatives of any foreign government—be it British or American. White frontiersmen also had little reason to see the power of governments and laws as positive forces in their lives. Virginia's confusing land laws and the state's ragged support of Kentuckians' wars with the British and Indians in the Old Northwest (epitomized by the dealings of various governors with George Rogers Clark) alienated many residents of the Ohio Valley. Above all, the United States government dealt with white settlers in the Ohio Valley in almost exclusively negative ways: it forbade them to settle in certain places; it attacked their relations with Indians; it criticized their collective character; and it seemed most eager to respond to the demands of easterners with interests in the West. Government was not an institution on which frontiersmen were inclined to rely.[26]

In sum, the world of the hunters was personal, unspecialized, and marked by unpredictable bursts of danger and long periods of boredom. Their world revolved around a network of family and friends, not banks, churches, schools, or governments. On the frontier the abilities to fight, to defend one's family, and to shoot straight and accurately determined a man's self-worth and reputation. Men and women in the undeveloped West did not embrace bourgeois values of self-control, delayed gratification, and internalization of emotions because they were ignorant or defiant but because such things had little meaning in their world.[27]

To a large extent Indian males shared the values of the white hunters—or vice versa. Frontier warfare, therefore, became a masculine sport on the grand scale. Whites and Indians immediately reciprocated for any attack on their families or their reputations. Murders of whites were punished by murders of Indians. Only in this context can we begin to understand the slaughter of the defenseless Christian Indians in the Moravian mission at Gnadenhutten in 1782 by whites from Pennsylvania. Men on both sides acquired prestige by collecting scalps. Torture became an extended test of one's manhood. Witness the Indian admiration for men like Col. William Crawford, who survived long hours of mutilation and taunting before he was burned to death in 1782. To die honorably, even by fire, was far preferable to living in shame.[28]

Ultimately, of course, what Indians and white frontiersmen were fighting about was land. But more specifically, they were fighting for control of a certain kind of environment. They were not struggling to guide the development of the Ohio Valley but to survive in a difficult world. Society in the Ohio Valley in the 1780s was "primitive" in the sense that it was local, that it lacked economic complexity, that it did not have permanent buildings and elaborate towns, that institutions were weak, and that there was little interest in the high arts and social interdependence. But it was not primitive in the sense that it was disorganized or anarchic. Frontier society was a world of highly developed rituals and values. It was a world that was foreign to the authors of the Northwest Ordinance; it made them uncomfortable. But we can call it anarchic and backward only if we accept their definitions of anarchy and backwardness.

And, of course, Americans in the twentieth century generally do. Why? Largely because the world of the frontier has disappeared, taking with it styles of behavior that would be out of place in a modern, urban, industrial economy. Frederick Jackson Turner and other historians have long argued that the frontier indelibly shaped the American experience. To a significant degree, they were right. But just as important is the degree to which the expanding world of the market—national and international economic interdependence, gentility and piety, schools and churches, and the authority of the national government—overran and destroyed local societies that differed from it.

The authors of the Northwest Ordinance were not in any way tyrannical. After all, they created a territorial system under which colonies could become equal partners in the American Union with the same rights, privileges, and duties as the original thirteen states. Still, it is important to remember that they used their power to insure that the colonies would only become states when their laws and institutions clearly reflected the values and structures of civilized society as these men defined it.

Congressmen began serious consideration of a territorial system in 1783–84 when Virginia finally agreed to cede its claim to the lands north of the Ohio River. Their deliberations resulted in the Ordinance of 1784, the precursor of the Northwest Ordinance. (See Appendix.) Traditionally, scholars have attributed the ideas and text of the

1784 act to Thomas Jefferson. But the ordinance was not the work of one man; it was an outgrowth of an old debate about American expansion.

Efforts to develop a systematic western policy under the control of some sort of central authority began as early as the French and Indian War of 1754–63. In 1754 delegates from several colonies attending a meeting in Albany, New York, advocated the creation of a "general government" to coordinate a common defense. Drawn up by Benjamin Franklin, the Albany Plan put effective control of western settlement and development in the hands of this "general government." While opposition from both colonial and British authorities doomed the plan, the desire for greater control over western expansion did not die with it.[29] The British Proclamation of 1763, which attempted to limit Anglo-American migration beyond the crest of the Appalachians, called for settlement of new territories in stages and asserted the authority of the British government in London over land purchases and grants beyond the restricted boundaries of individual colonies.

Even as they fought for freedom from the British government that issued the Proclamation of 1763, many officers of the American army kept alive the notion of a coordinated, controlled development of the West during the American Revolution. Disturbed by their perception of moral decline and political chaos in the 1780s and frustrated by Congress's inability to pay them, officers such as Timothy Pickering and Rufus Putnam developed plans for a slow, systematic occupation of the trans-Appalachian West under the authority of the United States government.[30]

Many congressmen in the 1780s agreed with the officers' demand for coordinated western policy. One of the problems with the Articles of Confederation (the document under which the national government operated between 1777 and 1789) was its failure to provide for western expansion; the states simply refused to surrender that power to a central authority that people in the 1770s fundamentally distrusted. By the mid-1780s, however, many Americans were more afraid of anarchy (symbolized by the rough and ready behavior of defiant frontiersmen) than a central authority. Their fears led to the creation of a stronger national government in the Constitution of 1787; they also led to the articulation of a more forceful western policy. Congressmen accepted what Robert Berkhofer has called "the principle that . . . statehood must evolve from a previous condition of subordination."[31] In so doing they followed a line of reasoning about the development of the West which had been evolving for at least thirty years.

The Ordinance of 1784 outlined a movement toward eventual statehood through a series of stages. In the beginning a territory could receive the right from Congress to establish a temporary government, but its citizens had to adopt the constitution and laws of one of the thirteen original states. When the territory had 20,000 free inhabitants, Congress could grant them the power to call a representative convention to devise a permanent constitution and to elect a non-voting delegate to send to Congress. In the final stage the territory, having achieved a population equal to that of the smallest of the original thirteen states, could be given equal status within the Confederation by vote of Congress.[32]

Despite the fact that the Ordinance of 1784 allowed for participation in the process of becoming a state by residents of the territory involved, the document was a thoroughgoing assertion of the sovereignty of Congress in the Northwest. No new state could be admitted to the Union without the express permission of Congress. By forcing the territories to adopt one of the existing state constitutions during the first stage of government, moreover, the Ordinance of 1784 required that eastern, not western, ideas and political structures be the models of the future state governments.

The Northwest Ordinance of 1787, adopted some three years later after repeated failures by Congress, the United States Army, and other government officials to assert the sovereignty of Congress over the Indians and whites on the frontier, was much more specific and restrictive in prescribing the evolution from colony to state. The 1787 document was essentially an elaboration of the May 9, 1786, report of a committee appointed to review territorial government under the direction of James Monroe. Congressmen debated the report, and a July 1786 revision of it, for a year. On May 9, 1787, a final draft of the report passed its second reading. A final vote was delayed until July because of the desire of several members to attend the Constitutional Convention in Philadelphia and the wish of others to go on vacation. On July 9 Congress sent the plan to a committee headed by Nathan Dane of Massachusetts for a final reworking, which included determining the number of states to be created from the territory and increasing both the restrictions on those states and the list of civil liberties granted in the articles. After adding the famous article prohibiting slavery, Congress unanimously passed the Ordinance on Friday, July 13.[33]

The Ordinance of 1787 simply enhanced a policy of congressional guidance and control that was already present in the Ordinance of 1784. The differences in the two documents were largely in the realm of details. In terms of fundamental policy they were very similar. Both committed the United States to a colonial policy that allowed for the orderly assimilation of new territories. But in both admission to the Union was contingent upon the adoption of a government and a society acceptable to Congress. However democratic the end result of the Northwest Ordinance may have been, the process it established as a means to that end was very restrictive and undemocratic.

Precisely what kind of government did Congress mean by republican? And, in a larger sense, what kind of world did it intend the new states to be? At the heart of the Ordinance of 1787 were the famous six articles guaranteeing, among other things, freedom of religion, public education, and the prohibition of slavery. The authors of the Ordinance directed that these "Articles shall be considered as Articles of compact between the Original States and the People and States in the said territory, and forever remain unalterable, unless by common consent."[34] In the nineteenth and twentieth centuries Americans came to revere these provisions as virtually unique guarantees of rights to peoples of a colony. What other country has been so generous in extending the privileges of full citizenship to residents of subordinate territories? Certainly not the English government in the seventeenth and eighteenth centuries; the American colonists had to fight a war to win their freedom and to exercise full sovereignty. Not so the settlers of the Old Northwest: the July 1787 Ordinance provided for "extending the fundamental principles of Civil and religious liberty, which form the basis wheron these Republics [meaning the thirteen original states], their laws and constitutions are erected."[35] From the perspective of the casual modern observer what is striking is the degree to which Congress surrendered power to the people of the territory.

But from the perspective of the frontier in 1787 the opposite is true. What is paramount in the articles is the degree to which Congress asserted its power over territorial residents. The Northwest Ordinance granted rights under certain conditions and promised full citizenship only under certain circumstances. The emphasis was on the maintenance of social order by the supreme authority of the government of the United States in order to fashion a society more in keeping with the new American order than the one already in existence in the Ohio Valley.

In announcing the purpose of the articles the authors of the Ordinance described them as constituting a "compact" subject to change only "by common consent." Yet at no time were the citizens of the territory to be asked for their opinion on the articles. The Northwest Ordinance was simply an act of Congress; unlike the Constitution of the United States, it was never ratified by any convention or group of people outside of the government. It was only fundamental law because Congress said it was. In no sense

can it be construed as a "compact." Congress had no intention of consulting frontiersmen or Indians on how to
govern the Northwest Territory. Eventually, the residents of
the territory would be able to create their own states; but
those entities would have to be "Republican, and in conformity to the principles contained in these Articles."[36] In
other words, territorial residents were free to form their
own governments only within parameters laid down by the
sovereign authority of the national government.

The articles of the Ordinance, moreover, prescribed
the establishment of a society that was in many ways the
antithesis of that already on the frontier. The famous guarantee of freedom of religion was reserved to those people
who behaved "in a peaceable and orderly manner."[37] And,
with regard to Article Two, as crucial as the protection of
contracts and property and the establishment of legal pro-
cedures were in an interdependent, impersonal capitalistic
society, they had little relevance in the local, personal, less
developed cultures of frontier hunters. What Article Two
essentially accomplished was the replacement of community decision-making processes and personal resolutions
of conflicts with the authority of the law and courts (pre-
sided over by nationally appointed judges). Private property was made sacrosanct in ways that mattered far more to
eastern speculators (like members of the Ohio Company of
Associates) than frontier residents. While admirable in
retrospect, Article Three's commitment to education was
less a grant of a right to individuals than a reminder of the
government's obligation to develop responsible citizens by
insuring the inculcation of the "Religion, Morality, and
knowledge" so important "to good government."[38] In
short, congressmen saw religion, law, and schools as bul-
warks of a new social order in the Ohio Valley.

In the same article and in the same spirit, Congress
also announced that "the utmost good faith shall always be
observed towards the Indians." By asserting that the lands
of the natives would never be taken "without their consent," Congress was promising a rational, legal, and more

equitable approach to the issue of the Indians. It clearly rejected the often violent system of reciprocity in which white frontiersmen and Indians dealt with each other. According to Secretary of War Henry Knox, the national government would have to "keep them both in awe by a strong hand, and compel them to be moderate and just."[39]

Congress's assertion of its power was even stronger in Article Four. The locus of sovereignty was clearly defined. Forever subject to the constitutions and laws of the United States, the people of the states created from the Northwest Territory could "never interfere with the primary disposal of the Soil," which was forever the property of "the United States in Congress Assembled."[40]

Finally, Congress's attack on slavery, which existed in the Old Northwest before and after 1787, north of the Ohio River was implicitly part of its general assault on frontier society. In recent years historians have begun to identify antislavery sentiments with people intimately involved in the growth of international market capitalism in the late eighteenth and early nineteenth centuries. Opposition to slavery, which was the most brutal of institutional restraints on individuals, was part of a general opposition to any form of control over human beings. Slavery, Eugene D. Genovese, among others, has contended, was an integral part of a pre-capitalistic, patriarchal society. At the core of capitalism was an impersonal labor system that thrived on specialization. Slavery was incompatible with capitalism because it epitomized face-to-face, vertical relationships. The Northwest Ordinance's feeble (but significant) attack on slavery was not simply an effort to free blacks; it was part of the whole document's concern with replacing one set of values, one set of customs, with another.[41]

Of course the new ways of doing things laid out in the Northwest Ordinance did not conquer the frontier immediately. The Indians of the region, who suffered a major defeat at the Battle of Fallen Timbers in 1794, were nonetheless a major presence in the Ohio Valley until after the War of 1812. The French residents of Vincennes and Kaskaskia were eventually absorbed into American society, but it took years to resolve their tangled land claims. And the defense of local autonomy among Americans on the frontier provoked by the extension of national authority to the Northwest would become a basic component of statehood movements in Ohio and Indiana.

Nonetheless, the Ordinance of 1787 marked the beginning of a significant transformation of the economic and social structures of the Ohio Valley. While it promised territorial residents the eventual exercise of the full rights and privileges of American citizens, it did so only by preemptively defining the cultural context in which they could be enjoyed. Without consulting frontier residents, the Ordinance proclaimed the end of the world of the hunter, of the frontier society of Indians and whites. In its place it created a government and a society committed to national authority, to the rule of law and the protection of private property, to rationality and morality as they were understood in New York and Philadelphia, and to the values and structures of the expanding capitalist markets of the North Atlantic world. At least in the Old Northwest, the American Empire of Liberty was dedicated to the proposition that the kind of society which existed on the frontier in the 1780s was unworthy of the new United States.

The Vote and the Voters: July 13, 1787

BY

ROBERT M. TAYLOR, JR.

 THE NORTHWEST ORDINANCE, passed on July 13, 1787, with one dissenting vote, proved to be the last piece of major legislation acted upon by the Confederation Congress.[1] From May 25 of that year the nation's attention had been riveted on the Constitutional Convention underway in Philadelphia. A number of congressmen, elected as delegates to the convention, were in Philadelphia rather than New York, participating in what was generally considered to be the more exciting and significant arena, where an effort had begun to "render the federal constitution adequate to the exigencies of government and the preservation of the Union."[2] Among the congressmen attending the convention were such luminaries as Alexander Hamilton, Rufus King, Charles Pinckney, and James Madison. They joined George Washington, Gouverneur Morris, Benjamin Franklin, Edmund Randolph, and other prominent figures. It is this highly regarded collection of delegates, an "assembly of demigods" as Thomas Jefferson put it, plus the convention's sublime purpose and the image of a Confederation government in its twilight days that, in comparison, has put a stamp of mediocrity on the congressional remnant that voted for the Ordinance. As one

history textbook in the 1970s put it: "Indeed, the caliber of the delegates was the highest America had to offer, in striking contrast to the composition of the Confederation Congress then sitting in New York,"[3] a Congress, according to another source, which was "discredited, incompetent, senile and worse."[4]

One of the problems with observations of this sort, that in effect impute a second-rate status to the congressional body, is that they cast a shadow unfairly on the merits of the Ordinance itself. The assumption is that the congressmen in New York, who completed the legislation and pushed it through, comprised an inferior lot, the best and the brightest having removed to Philadelphia. As a result, in this view, the Ordinance lacks a deftness and sagacity that fundamental law should have and that greater intellects (presumably those in Philadelphia) could have given it.

What if, however, on closer look, we find that the differences between the two groups have been exaggerated? Then this argument against the Ordinance begins to unravel; Congress shows itself worthy in its production of an admirable bill; and those responsible for its composition and passage can be praised for their accomplishment. In other words, the profile of Congress is redrawn, and the Ordinance is viewed in a new and more favorable light.

Of course, it is not necessarily clear that there was a direct relationship between the abilities of those who voted for the Ordinance and the quality of the document itself. Only a small portion of the legislators had anything to do with its creation. The document was a product of the distillation of ideas that took place over many years, including contributions from several of the leading figures at the Constitutional Convention. Yet, as long as there is believed to be some link between the nature of the Ordinance and a lackluster Congress, then there is some justification for using a collective biography of the congressmen to test this assumption.

The Constitutional Convention depleted the congressional ranks in New York and led to problems in securing quorums for legislative action. Only eight of thirteen states had delegations present on July 13 to vote on the Ordinance. Five of the states and eleven of the eighteen legislators represented the South. Conspicuously absent among the northern states with close western ties were Connecticut and Pennsylvania. As it was, with each state having but one vote, a negative decision by two states could have nullified the act.[5] Among the representatives at that historic count only one, Richard Henry Lee of Virginia, probably would receive a flicker of recognition today. Still, upon examining the careers of Lee and his fellow congressmen, even in a cursory fashion, it becomes clear that while we may be unfamiliar with the names of those who passed the Ordinance, as a group they share many attributes with the delegates to the Constitutional Convention.

Much has been made of the youthfulness of the convention's delegates, whose average age was forty-two. Yet eight of the eighteen men voting on the Ordinance were in their thirties, and the group as a whole averaged forty-three years.[6] Occupationally, the two bodies also compared favorably; most in both groups were lawyers, and the large majority of the remaining members were either merchants or farmers. In addition, as would be the case in this time period, at least half of the members of both aggregations had prior military service.

While the delegates to the convention brought with them a wealth of governmental experience and would gain more in positions held under the new government, the congressmen who voted on the Ordinance exhibited a comparable history of and dedication to public service. Two of the latter signed the Declaration of Independence: Abraham Clark of New Jersey and Richard Henry Lee of Virginia. All but one of the voters had held, or would hold, a state office. Nathaniel Mitchell of Delaware, for example, would be elected that state's governor in 1805. Seven of the eighteen voters would go on to be members of their respective state conventions that ratified the Constitution.

Three of the voters performed the duties of a major officer in the Confederation Congress: Richard Henry Lee was president in 1784; Samuel Holten of Massachusetts was president pro tempore in 1785; and William Grayson of Virginia sat as temporary president in 1787 for the absent Arthur St. Clair. Seven of the eighteen Ordinance voters accepted federal appointments, the most consequential positions being filled by William Blount of North Carolina, who became governor of the "Territory South of the River Ohio," and Benjamin Hawkins of the same state, who worked as Indian agent for the same territory. Three of the congressmen in New York would be chosen as presidential electors. Finally, in terms of percentages, both groups would be almost equally represented in future congresses; twenty-eight of fifty-five convention delegates and nine of eighteen Ordinance voters would later serve as congressmen under the new Constitution. While no prospective United States presidents, vice-presidents, or Supreme Court justices sat in New York's congressional chambers, as were present in Philadelphia to debate a new frame of government, extensive public service in elective or appointive positions characterized both bodies.

A case can be made, however, that disparities in nativity and education suggest that convention members enjoyed a broader perspective, a cosmopolitanism, a set of richer experiences, which translated into their document. Almost a tenth of the convention delegates were foreign born, while all the congressmen were native to America. Over half of the men in attendance at Philadelphia had college training. Many had taught or occupied administrative posts in educational institutions. Only three of the eighteen congressmen in New York had college degrees (yet three other congressmen had studied in England and one, William Grayson of Virginia, held a law degree from Oxford).

Evidently the Philadelphia delegation was less provincial, more highly educated, and more likely to obtain high office. It is plausible, nevertheless, that with few exceptions any representative in the Confederation Congress at that time would have been a valuable asset at the Constitutional Convention. Many factors go into explaining why a person was in one place rather than another, elements not necessarily linked to reputation or mental ability. State and national politics, the individual's feelings about the need for or function of the Constitutional Convention, and the degree of genuine interest in the future of America's territories all played a part. In fact, six of the eighteen Ordinance voters were considered by their state legislatures as delegates to the convention, and five were elected. Melancthon Smith was one of seven nominated in New York, but he failed in the election. Virginia appointed Richard Henry Lee, but he declined to serve, as did Abraham Clark of New Jersey, who thought it inconsistent with his congressional duties. William Blount of North Carolina and William Pierce and William Few of Georgia attended the convention, but Pierce left before its conclusion.

Furthermore, it should be noted that six of the twelve congressional committee members who on February 21, 1787, called for a Constitutional Convention were present for the Ordinance vote. Nathan Dane, who had considerable responsibility for writing the Ordinance and who cast a vote for it, was on that committee and wrote the preamble and resolution calling for the convention.[7] Moreover, it is abundantly clear that much communication took place between members of both bodies as they deliberated their respective objectives.[8] Finally, before concluding that the convention possessed America's most capable minds and effective leaders, we should recall that such grand figures as John Jay, John Adams, Thomas Jefferson, Samuel Adams, and Patrick Henry were not participants at the Philadelphia gathering.

In short, the quality of both aggregations was imposing. If the convention was one, in the words of James MacGregor Burns, "of the well-bred, the well-fed, the well-read, and the well-wed" so too was that Congress that framed the Ordinance.[9] The contrast between the two groups has been overstated. The Congress that enacted the Ordinance was not a disreputable and decrepit body, but rather a group of able legislators who had profound political and ideological interests in sanctioning the Ordinance.

From The Pennſylvania Packet

The subscribers take this method to inform all officers and soldiers who served in the late war, and who are by an ordinance of the honorable Congress to receive certain tracts of land in the Ohio Country; and also, all other good citizens who wish to become adventurers in that delightful region; that from personal inspection, together with other incontestible evidence, they are fully satisfied that the lands in that quarter are of a much better quality than any other known to New–England people; that the climate, seasons, produce, & c. are in fact equal to the most flattering accounts which have ever been published of them—that being determined to become purchasers, and to prosecute a settlement in this country—and desirous of forming a general association with those who entertain the same ideas—they beg leave to propose the following plan, viz That an association by the name of the Ohio Company, be formed of all such as wish to become purchasers, &c. in that country . . .

Rufus Putman
Benjamin Tupper

Rutland, Jan. 10th, 1786

An announcement placed on February 13, 1786, to recruit stockholders for the Ohio Company of Associates. (Indiana Historical Society)

Marietta, Ohio, named for Queen Marie Antoinette of France and founded April 7, 1788, by the Ohio Company of Associates, was the first colony planted in the territory after the passage of the Northwest Ordinance. [Georges Henri Victor Collot, **A Journey in North America** *(Paris, 1826).]*

A French house in the Illinois country
as sketched by Georges Henri Victor Collot in the mid-1790s. Called "Poteuaux
in terra" (post in earth), the house had a steep roof and a covered four-sided
porch that provided protection from snow, rain, and heat.

(Engraving by Pierre Alexandre (?) Tardieu after the drawing by Collot.
By permission of the Harvard College Library.)

Social life of the early French settlers of Illinois.
(Indiana Historical Society)

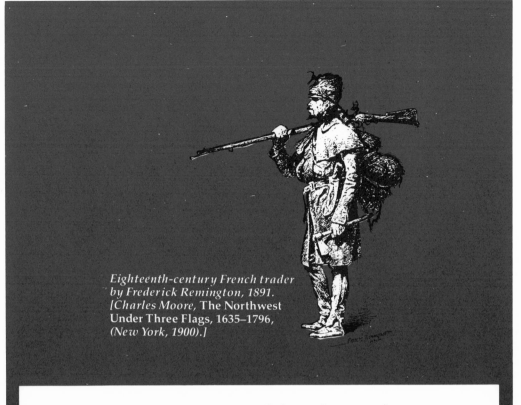

Eighteenth-century French trader by Frederick Remington, 1891. [Charles Moore, The Northwest Under Three Flags, 1635–1796, (New York, 1900).]

From The Pennſylvania Packet

Charlestown (Mass.) April 14

Congress, with a press, during the life of paper money, did wonders; they have had the power of emitting bills, and borrowing money, without funds to gain credit—of raising an army and equipping a navy, without the means of building a ship or subsisting a soldier—of sending ambassadors, who divulge our distress abroad, and render our poverty more splendidly conspicuous—making treaties which they cannot enforce the execution of; and finally, they present themselves a spectacle of ludicrous, that we cannot help being diverted at our own calamities.

The amelioration of a constitution, founded on such false and incompatible principles, seems to us in every view impossible; but expedients proposed, which require the unanimous concurrence of thirteen separate legislatures, differing in interests, distinct in habits, and opposite from prejudices, have so repeatedly failed, that they no longer furnish a ray of hope. We pray, therefore, for the day when we shall see a *national constitution*, fit composed of the best and ablest men in the union, a majority of whom shall be invested with the power of altering it. It is now so bad, as to defy the malice of fortune and ingenuity to make it worse.

Correspondence on the weaknesses of Congress under the Articles of Confederation printed in the May 19, 1786, issue. (Indiana Historical Society)

Nathan Dane (1752–1835), born into a large family of an Ipswitch, Massachusetts, farmer, went on to graduate from Harvard, publish legal tomes, and serve in the Massachusetts and the Confederation legislatures. He is generally thought to be the chief author of the Northwest Ordinance. [John Fiske, *The Critical Period of American History*, 1783–1789 (Boston: 1896).]

Ireland-born Charles Thomson (1729–1824), whose name appears at the end of the Northwest Ordinance document, was secretary of a succession of Congresses from 1774 to 1789. [Benson J. Lossing, *Harper's Popular Cyclopedia of United States History . . .*, vol. 2 (New York, 1881).]

On passing the above Ordinance the yeas and nays being required by M[r] [Abraham] Yates

Massachusetts		Virginia	
M[r] Holten	ay }ay	M[r] Grayson	ay
M[r] Dane	ay	M[r] R H Lee	ay }ay
New York		M[r] Carrington	ay
M[r] Smith	ay	North Carolina	
M[r] Haring	ay }ay	M[r] Blount	ay }ay
M[r] Yates	no	M[r] Hawkins	ay
New Jersey		South Carolina	
M[r] Clarke	ay }ay	M[r] Kean	ay }ay
M[r] Schurman	ay	M[r] Huger	ay
Delaware		Georgia	
M[r] Kearny	ay }ay	M[r] Few	ay }ay
M[r] Mitchell	ay	M[r] Pierce	ay

So it was resolved in the affirmative.

The vote on the Northwest Ordinance, July 13, 1787. Each state had one vote. [*Journal of the Continental Congress 1774-1789*, vol. 32, 1787, January 17–July 20 (Washington, 1936).]

Manasseh Cutler (1742–1823), Congregational clergyman, physician, botanist, and congressman, helped draw up the constitution of the Ohio Company of Associates and played a key role in lobbying for the associates in the halls of Congress. [William Parker Cutler and Julia Perkins Cutler, *Life Journals and Correspondence of Rev. Manasseh Cutler, LL.D.*, vol. 1 (Cincinnati, 1888).]

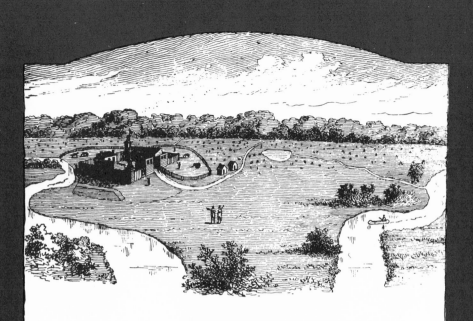

From The Pennſylvania Packet

Philadelphia, March 4

The various letters lately published, said to be received from gentlemen in the back country, stating the great probability of an Indian war in the spring, merit serious consideration. It is hard to suppose that any person would be villainous enough to forge them, merely to spread an alarm. And if they are well founded, it would be a fatal mistake to defer making preparations, until the Indians commenced depredations. The retention of the frontier posts by the British, and the movements of the Indians, seem pregnant with dangers to the confederation.

Philadelphia, June 20

Letters since published, said to be from persons in the Western country, and which so delightfully prognosticate all the horrors of an Indian war, are suspected not to have originated quite so far westerly but are fabricated in some of our *cities* of *refinement,* (perhaps New York) for the purpose of more easily making a valuable appropriation of an extensive tract of land, in the kindliest clime, and of the most luxuriant soil in the universe—and indeed the policy is well adapted to the design, for the terror of the savages would deter the people of this country almost from Paradise itself.

Persistent rumors of Indian uprisings on the frontier made interesting copy for eastern newspapers and led to speculations on the authenticity and authorship of the stories, as seen in these items from 1786. (Indiana Historical Society)

Arthur St. Clair (1736–1818),
first governor of the Northwest Territory.
[William Henry Smith, **The St. Clair Papers: The Life and Public Services of**
Arthur St. Clair *(Cincinnati, 1882).]*

A late nineteenth-century depiction of Indian life a century earlier.
[A Popular History of Indiana (Indianapolis, 1891).]

The seal of the Northwest Territory
as seen on the facade of Ohio State University's William Oxley Thomp-
son Library in Columbus. The seal's major elements were apparently
borrowed from South Carolina's seal. The latin motto means "Having
fallen, it has planted a better one."
   [Edgar C. Reinke, "Meliorem Lapsa Locavit: An Intriguing Puzzle
   Solved," Ohio History 94 (1985), 68-74. (Ohio Historical Society)]

The Northwest Ordinance:
An Annotated Text

An Ordinance for the government of the territory of the United States North west of the river Ohio. [1]

[SECTION 1]

Be it ordained by the United States in Congress Assembled that the said territory for the purpose of temporary government be one district, subject however to be divided into two districts as future circumstances may in the opinion of Congress make it expedient

THOUGH AGONIZINGLY weak-willed at times and lacking a clear constitutional right to command, the Confederation Congress was frequently compelled by urgent matters to overstep its stated authority and create important legislation. This legislation often took the form of an ordinance. The Northwest Ordinance was by far the most significant of these "extra-legal" enactments. By declaring this written instrument an ordinance, Congress attached to it a particular legal property. It was certainly not a constitution, though some writers have understandably confused the two kinds of documents. One obvious reason that the Northwest Ordinance was not considered a constitution was that Congress had no intention of having the legis-

lation undergo a ratification process. It was, as Andrew
Cayton has said in the foregoing essay, simply an act of
Congress. Still, its framers viewed it as a special kind of act
by labeling it an ordinance. Today the term is commonly
used to mean a law enacted by a municipal body, not one
passed by a state or federal legislature. The idea that an
ordinance had restricted application was familiar to eighteenth-century legislators who drew a distinction between
public or general laws that affected the entire nation and
edicts such as an ordinance that were pertinent only to a
section of the country.

Members of Congress also seem to have understood
the degree of impermanence implied in the designation.
Among the various meanings for ordinance in early English canon is that of a temporary act amendable by Parliament, as opposed to an "act" of Parliament which was a
perpetual law not to be changed except by consent of the
Crown and both houses of Parliament. By the late eighteenth century the distinctions between an ordinance and
other forms of legislation had blurred somewhat. English
law dictionaries fused ordinance with decree, statute, or
law.[2] Still, at least one English dictionary, published in
1790, referred to an ordinance as a temporary act alterable
by the House of Commons.[3] In the Northwest Ordinance
this connotation of temporality is evident in that part that
comes before the six "articles of compact." This initial portion of the Ordinance, which is essentially the plan for the
territory's government, was considered changeable by
some contemporaries. Because its provisions did not come
under the heading of articles of compact, which were considered inviolable, it seemed the document's most vulner-
able part, that which could be remodeled.

Notwithstanding the limited nature of the Ordinance,
it bore the earmarks of a constitution, and for the most part
it functioned as a constitution, or perhaps better stated, a
"fundamental ordinance" for the Northwest Territory.
Black's Law Dictionary says as much in defining "Ordinance" as a name "given to certain enactments, more gen-

eral in their character than ordinary statutes, and serving as organic laws, yet not exactly to be called 'constitutions.' Such was the 'Ordinance' . . . enacted by Congress in 1787."[4]

Congress provided for the future division of the Northwest Territory if circumstances warranted. It was not clear in 1787 how quickly the territory would be settled or how soon population pressures would result in new states being formed. Until these pressures developed, Congress left the door open for it to partition the territory for ease of government, perhaps as a step prior to the awarding of statehood. Why Congress thought in terms of two territorial districts is not entirely clear, but two did exist in 1800 when it created the Indiana Territory three years before Ohio became a state.

RMT

[SECTION 2]

Be it ordained by the authority aforesaid, that the estates both of resident and non resident proprietors in the said territory dying intestate shall descend to and be distributed among their children and the descendants of a deceased child in equal parts; the descendants of a deceased child or grand child to take the share of their deceased parent in equal parts among them; and where there shall be no children or descendants then in equal parts to the next of kin in equal degree—and among collaterals the children of a deceased brother or sister of the intestate shall have in equal parts among them their deceased parent's share & there shall in no case be a distinction between kindred of the whole & half blood; saving in all cases to the widow of the intestate her third part of the real estate for life, and one third part of the personal estate: and this law relative to descents and dower shall remain in full force until altered by the legislature of the district. And until the governor & judges shall adopt laws as herein after mentioned estates in the said territory may be devised or bequeathed by wills in writing signed and sealed by him or her in whom the estate be, (being of full age,) and attested by three witnesses, and real estates may be conveyed by lease and release or bargain and sale signed, sealed and delivered by the person being of full age in whom the estate may be and attested by two witnesses provided such wills be duly proved and such conveyances be acknowledged or the execution thereof duly proved and be recorded within one year after proper magistrates, courts and registers shall be appointed for that purpose and personal property may be transferred by delivery saving however to the french and canadian inhabitants & other settlers of the Kaskaskies, Saint Vincents, and the neighboring villages who have heretofore professed themselves citizens of Virginia, their laws and customs now in force among them relative to the descent & conveyance of property

This section of the Ordinance forbade the application of primogeniture, the right of inheritance belonging exclusively to the eldest son, in cases where the deceased had no recorded will, thus dying intestate. It also details the manner of distribution to heirs of real and personal property.

The law of primogeniture did not arise in the Western world until emperors and kings began to create titles of nobility. Then, to preserve the integrity of the position and to see that it descended to the eldest son alone, laws were enacted to prevent properties from being partitioned.[5] Besides appearing in the highest classes of society, impartible succession, or primogeniture, appeared among the villeins, or peasants. The economic basis of this practice was clearly the endeavor to maintain the peasant's landholding intact and therefore sufficient to sustain the whole of his family and still meet the heavy burden owed to the lord and in turn to the king.

It was not until 1540 that it was possible for a man to make disposition of any of his real estate by will. Thus, until only some sixty years before the first settlement in Virginia, no Englishman had the right to dispose of any real property belonging to him at the time of his death other than to his eldest son. It had been possible, however, since about the year 1200 to transfer property during one's lifetime.

The American colonies in which primogeniture existed as law and custom were New York, New Jersey, Virginia, North and South Carolina, and Georgia. Some colonies passed laws relating to distribution in intestate estates, but in most the English statutes were considered sufficient. As early as 1705 the Virginia Assembly passed a law that significantly modified the status of primogeniture. Further acts of 1727, 1751, 1752, 1765, and, finally, Thomas Jefferson's bill of 1776 in essence finished off what had long been law and custom.[6]

Why was this provision on the descent and conveyance of property written into the Ordinance? It seems redundant given the climate of opinion on the matter, reflected by Virginia's influential ruling a decade earlier. Too, the nation's abundance of land made it unnecessary to assure descent of real property to the eldest son or any son. Moreover, as Jack Eblen has observed, the section, as a law, simply did not belong in a document that purported to have a constitutional or fundamental character. Eblen goes on to explain that Nathan Dane, the author of the section, thought that this particular American practice of equal distribution of estates to heirs was an essential lesson in republican principles; one that should be spelled out because he feared that residents in the western country might entertain incompatible ideas and institutions.[7] In other words, the section had a specific didactic function.

Whether one could understand it after reading it was another matter. As Phillip R. Shriver puts it, "This was legalese that only a lawyer could love or even read." Dane cast the section into two long sentences of over 170 words each just to say that primogeniture would not be allowed in the new territory. To Shriver, this turgid style of presentation, foremostly illustrated in this section, has been one of the reasons the public has neglected the Northwest Ordinance.[8]

WH

[**SECTIONS 3–5**]

Be it ordained by the authority aforesaid that there shall be appointed from time to time by Congress a governor, whose commission shall continue in force for the term of three years, unless sooner revoked by Congress: he shall reside in the district and have a freehold estate therein, in one thousand acres of land while in the exercise of his office. There shall be appointed from time to time by Congress a secretary, whose commission shall continue in force for four years, unless sooner revoked: he shall reside in the district and have a freehold estate therein in five hundred acres of land while in the exercise of his office; It shall be his duty to keep and preserve the acts and laws passed by the legislature and the public records of the district and the proceedings of the governor in his executive department and transmit authentic copies of such acts & proceedings every six months to the Secretary of Congress. There shall also be appointed a court to consist of three judges any two of whom to form a court, who shall have a common law jurisdiction and reside in the district and have each therein a freehold estate in five hundred acres of land while in the exercise of their offices, and their commissions shall continue in force during good behaviour.

The governor, and judges or a majority of them shall adopt and publish in the district such laws of the original states criminal and civil as may be necessary and best suited to the circumstances of the district and report them to Congress from time to time, which laws shall be in force in the district until the organization of the general assembly therein, unless disapproved of by Congress; but afterwards the legislature shall have authority to alter them as they shall think fit.

A governor, a secretary, and three judges comprised the governmental structure of the Northwest Territory. The governor was charged with several responsibilities: territorial administrator, militia commander, public land officer, and superintendent of Indian affairs. Arthur St. Clair was appointed by the Confederation Congress as the first governor.[9] Although the governor shared lawmaking powers with the three judges, he had almost dictatorial powers as the chief executive and militia commander in a governmental system that lacked a formal legislature in its initial stage. Many of the constituents believed the governor's office had too little regard for their democratic aspirations. St. Clair, for example, viewed them as "indigent and ignorant" frontiersmen who, he insisted, were too far removed from the national seat of government to be impressed with the power of the national government. St. Clair was certain that, if left to their own choices, the frontiersmen would select a "troublesome" form of government, such as democracy.[10] However, it should be remembered that St. Clair and others believed a strong, centralized government was imperative in a territory where great distances separated the settlements and where mere survival was a constant concern. The Northwest Ordinance's establishment of property requirements for officeholders suggests that the Confederation Congress wanted conservative landowners to administer the territory.

The territorial secretary assisted the governor with correspondence and record keeping and sent regular reports of the territorial executive proceedings to the nation's capital. The secretary's most important task (one not specifically mentioned in the Northwest Ordinance) was to assume the powers and duties of the governor when the latter was absent from the territory. Winthrop Sargent, the first secretary, filled in often for St. Clair since the governor was frequently away on official or personal business. Sargent and St. Clair got along well for over a decade, largely because they shared a distrust of frontiersmen. However, when Sargent left to become governor of the Mississippi Territory in 1798, St. Clair feared the politics of the new secretary, William Henry Harrison, and refused to allow Harrison to act in his absence.

Three judges worked with the governor to formulate territorial laws. They were not given the power to "make" laws—they could only "adopt" existing laws from the origi-

nal states and use them in the Northwest Territory. Feeling
severely restricted by this requirement, St. Clair and the
judges—Samuel Parsons, James Varnum, and John Symmes—agreed among themselves to modify the laws of
other states and add new laws to fit the frontier conditions,
as long as the laws remained true to the Constitution and
republican principles. The approved laws blended English
common law, colonial practice, Puritan punishments (including time in the stocks and whippings), and frontier
expediency. The earliest laws set up a territorial militia for
all males, established a territorial court system, and enu-
merated a list of crimes and punishments.

The governor and the judges met only a few days each
year to consider legislative matters. Although expected to
act jointly on legal considerations, the governor often offered his views and left the judges to deliberate, especially
on minor topics. For the first few years, the enacted laws
were read in the General Court, no stipulations having
been made for their publication or distribution throughout
the territory. By 1792 East Coast printers were publishing
the laws, and after 1795 Cincinnati took over the job. The
laws were revised and summarized in 1795 in what has
since become known as Maxwell's Code (taken from the
name of the Cincinnati printer).

JWM

[SECTION 6]

The governor for the time being shall be Commander in
chief of the Militia, appoint and commission all officers in
the same below the rank of general officers: All general
officers shall be appointed & commissioned by Congress.

This provision appears in the Northwest Ordinance in
the section delineating the powers of territorial governor.
When considered in light of the importance of the issue it
seeks to address (the role of the militia in the development
of the Northwest Territory and, indeed, the whole nation),
this section of the Ordinance is amazingly short. There is

no discussion of the size, composition, duties, or even mission of the militia, as one would expect from men who had just been through the most trying political and military experience of their lives. With the exception of congressional appointment of general officers (on whose duties or numbers the Ordinance makes no effort to elaborate), the territorial governor has all the power as the commander in chief.

In fact, the main difference between the provision governing the militia in the Ordinance and its counterpart in the Articles of Confederation, under which the nation still operated, was in the location of control. In the latter, control was vested in the state legislature (Articles Six and Seven). The states reserved the power to appoint their own officers at or below the rank of colonel.[11] The attempt of these provisions was to retain military power, at least in peacetime, at the state level. The fear was not one of an army per se, but of the potential uses of that army.

Most knowledgeable leaders recognized the need for at least a limited military force; the argument was over how much of this force would be local militia and how much would be national army. On the one hand, Antifederalists like Elbridge Gerry of Massachusetts fought successfully in 1781 and 1783 to restrict the military force to a militia organization, while others, like Alexander Hamilton of New York, continued to place reliance for national defense on a respectable standing army, with only a limited role for the militia.[12] Eventually, Hamilton and his allies were successful in making the military force more of a national instrument through the provisions in the Constitution dealing with that issue.[13] This success was due in no small part to the ideological shift in favor of more centralized government that took place in the new nation between the time of the Articles of Confederation and that of the Constitution.

One way in which this shift was manifested was through the provisions for the militia in the Northwest Ordinance. The closer resemblance of these to the Constitution than to the Articles of Confederation would at first appear inconsistent since the Ordinance was approved by the government operating under the latter. However, little is done in a vacuum, and the Ordinance is no exception. The document reflected in part the views of a group of land speculators, including Gen. Rufus Putnam, Rev. Manasseh Cutler, Samuel Parsons, and Rufus King (who introduced the call for the convention that produced the Constitution). All of these men were nationalists and favored central control of the military.[14] In addition, the Ordinance was written the same summer that saw the creation of the Constitution. The Confederation Congress must have been influenced by the swing toward more centralized power that affected the creation of that document.

Perhaps the greatest factor making possible national control of the territorial militia under the Ordinance was an event that shook the young nation to its core and called into serious question its ability to survive a national crisis under the Articles of Confederation. This event was Shays's Rebellion. The rebellion, which broke out in Massachusetts in September 1786, was precipitated by real grievances involving inequitable taxation, a commercial depression, and foreclosure of farms, mostly belonging to veterans.[15] The problems posed by a decentralized military power quickly became evident when the local militias were reluctant or, in some cases, refused to quell the outbreak. There was no reliable military power to enforce state or national law. Eventually, in early 1787, the governor mustered enough force from the eastern part of the state, combined with some loyal local militia, to do the job.[16] It was apparent, however, that the nation needed some kind of national force to impose order and to protect individuals from the lawless.

Shortly after this event the Ordinance appeared before the Congress for passage. It is not clear how much, if any, debate there was over the transfer of control of the militia from the local community to the national government, represented by the governor, but Congress, realizing that its days were numbered and stunned by its inability to deal with Shays's Rebellion, did not seem to put up much of a struggle over the issue.[17]

Part of the reason for placing all military power in the hands of the governor was expediency; it would have been difficult and inefficient to divide military authority in such a dangerous and sparsely settled area. Yet that same type of argument had failed the nationalists in 1783 when they attempted to maintain a strong standing army at the conclusion of the Revolution.[18] The underlying reason for the change in attitude was hard experience over the previous six years. The Antifederalists were, for the moment, in retreat, and those who advocated a stronger central government succeeded in their efforts. The most obvious example of the Federalist ascendancy is the Constitution, but the militia provision of the Northwest Ordinance is, in a smaller way, another.

RLS

[SECTION 7]

Previous to the organization of the general Assembly the governor shall appoint such magistrates and other civil officers in each county or township, as he shall find necessary for the preservation of the peace and good order in the same. After the general assembly shall be organized, the powers and duties of magistrates and other civil officers shall be regulated and defined by the said Assembly; but all magistrates and other civil officers, not herein otherwise directed shall during the continuance of this temporary government be appointed by the governor.

The Northwest Ordinance, as Don Fehrenbacher has bluntly described it, "was in some respects what Jefferson had intended, but...the first stage of the system can only be called autocratic, and the second stage, though it provided for a representative assembly, nevertheless included extensive checks on frontier democracy." The territorial governor enjoyed more power than the royal governors of colonial times and in fact possessed legal control of governmental machinery on a par with Napoleon's or Louis XVIII's, though of course the Ordinance's articles of compact provided protection to the personal and property rights of individuals.[19]

The term "magistrates" was perhaps a clue to the New England origins of the principal author of the Ordinance of 1787, and this section seems quite forthright in explaining its intent, "the preservation of the peace and good order" in the counties and townships. Liberty, equity, and justice may well have been goals of other sections of the Ordinance, but section seven took rather a New Englandish view of the frontier as a place peopled with tumultuous settlers likely to upset peace and good order unless restrained by civil officers responsible to the executive power only.[20]

Exclusive focus on this and similar clauses in the Ordinance will give rather a distorted picture of the law's intent, for this autocratic system would operate only until the second stage, when a popularly elected territorial assembly could regulate and define the powers of the governor's local officials and exercise other powers of representative self-government. Probably few people at the time thought the autocratic system would long rule, and the law itself made certain that no more than 5,000 Americans in five different and vast geographical areas would ever be subject to it, a maximum of 25,000 persons or six-tenths of one percent of the nation's population in 1790. Moreover, that number would not be subject to it all at one time (as the more easterly territories would reach statehood while the more westerly ones worked toward it under territorial rule). In other words, almost no one in government, no matter how Eastern and fearful of frontier disorder, contemplated subjecting even one percent of the population of the United States and its territories to rule without a local legislature for any period of time whatever.

It is little wonder, then, that in 1784 Thomas Jefferson himself had voted as a member of the Congress for an amendment to his liberal plan, which would have put the original settlers of a territory under the rule of Congress and magistrates appointed by Congress.[21] Nearly everyone recognized the necessity of a rather authoritarian system of government in the most primitive stages of settlement, and, conversely, almost no one wanted it to continue long. Even the second stage of limited colonial status, when the governor still appointed county and township officials (though their powers would be defined then by the assembly), was contemplated for no more than 300,000 people (that is, a maximum of 60,000 in each of the five territories before statehood), or less than eight percent of the total population of the country.[22]

Though it would be wrong to blink away the more authoritarian aspects of the Ordinance, it would be a greater mistake to focus on them exclusively. Their impact was carefully restricted to a small number of people under special conditions.

MEN

[SECTION 8]

For the prevention of crimes and injuries the laws to be adopted or made shall have force in all parts of the district and for the execution of process criminal and civil, the governor shall make proper divisions thereof, and he shall proceed from time to time as circumstances may require to lay out the parts of the district in which the indian titles shall have been extinguished into counties and townships subject however to such alterations as may thereafter be made by the legislature

Section five of the Ordinance provided the means by which civil and criminal laws could be adopted. Since the governor took the lead in the adoption of laws, most statutes reflected the origins of the governors. St. Clair's laws, for example, were influenced by his Pennsylvania background.[23] Laws regarding local government operations established General Courts of Quarter Sessions of the Peace,

County Courts of Common Pleas, Courts of Probate, and the Office of Sheriff, all of which seemed to be the only significant units of local government in the first stage of government.[24] Other laws regulated the militia, addressed the issue of marriage, and prescribed punishment for the crimes of treason, murder, manslaughter, arson, burglary, robbery, riots and unlawful assemblies, perjury, larceny, forgery, usurpation, assault and battery, fraudulent deeds, disobedience of children and servants, drunkenness, and improper and profane language, among others. Many of these reflected the severity of earlier New England codes.[25] This transference of New England laws to the West caused concern among governors and judges who "felt that none of the codes was fully suited to the needs of their territories."[26]

In adopting the new statutes, Governor St. Clair insisted, according to section eight, that all laws should apply equally throughout the territory: "Laws that are to run thro' so great an extent of Country...should be composed rather by an intermixture of those of all the original States.... An intermixture that would suit the whole Country, and tend to make the Inhabitants one People, would probably be obtained, without shocking too much the prejudices of any."[27]

While this might indicate St. Clair's desire for legal uniformity, the governor's stance actually limited lawmaking to very general statutes, applicable to the whole territory, even though some were "inappropriate for parts of the territory." Thus, St. Clair successfully prevented the adoption of specific laws to address particular conditions and needs and thereby limited the powers of local authorities and insured that his own executive powers in civil and criminal matters remained absolute.[28]

The attempt to establish a code of laws revealed a striking difference of opinion between St. Clair and the judges over the issue of "adopting" laws. St. Clair contended that the territorial judges could not assume original legislative authority, that both the governor and judges could only transfer statutes intact from other state codes and apply them to the entire territory, and that the governor ultimately retained an absolute power of veto. Any alteration of existing laws or creation of laws to meet specific needs, in St. Clair's opinion, would constitute law "making" and hence would be beyond the authority granted to either official, thereby almost insuring certain censure from Congress.[29] The judges, however, considered the governor as a coequal in legislative matters and claimed that territorial laws had to be consistent only with the republican principles of the original state codes.[30] In time, St. Clair acquiesced to permit some "original" legislation for specific territorial needs. Even though the laws were never officially approved by Congress, they apparently remained in force throughout the territory until the second stage of government was attained in 1795.

In an address before the territorial House of Representatives on September 25, 1799, Governor St. Clair emphasized the importance of uniform laws for the Northwest Territory: "The providing for, and the regulating the lives and morals of the present and of the rising generations...both here and hereafter, depend very much upon the spirit and genius of their laws."[31] But for St. Clair, a strong legal code was, in the words of Peter Onuf, the means of "underscoring the authority of the colonial government authorized by the Ordinance," the "degradation of citizen to state-less subject," and the elevation of the territorial governor to an autocratic ruler.[32]

The Ordinance of 1784 allowed the settlers themselves to divide territories into counties and townships in order to establish rudimentary local government.[33] In contrast, James Monroe's congressional report of May 9, 1786, which in its refined form became the Ordinance of 1787, made the entire Northwest Territory one administrative district overseen by a governor. The governor's powers included dividing the territory into counties and townships and appointing magistrates and civil officials to maintain order.[34] Once a territorial legislature was elected during the second stage of government, it assumed the power to alter boundaries and to regulate local officials.[35]

At the beginning of the first stage of territorial government, Governor St. Clair created several large counties and located seats of government close to the centers of population for "the prevention of crimes and the administration of justice."[36] He began on July 15, 1788, by establishing his administrative base at Marietta in Washington County (which embraced most of present-day Ohio) and appointing local officials.[37] In the ensuing years, as population concentrations arose at great distances from county seats, settlers petitioned the governor, or the governor himself perceived the need, to create new counties in order to facilitate the development of local governments.[38] In many instances, however, St. Clair resisted public pressure to create counties, arguing that the area did not possess sufficient numbers of settlers, that he knew relatively little about the character of the settlers, or that large counties minimized the cost of government.[39]

There was no smooth transition of county-making power into the second stage of territorial government. Near the adjournment of the general assembly's first session in 1799, St. Clair vetoed six legislative acts creating new counties, explaining that it was "the proper business of the Executive" to lay out counties and that the legislature could alter counties only with his approval and only after he had established them.[40] Furthermore, St. Clair argued that "this power might have been better vested in you, or in the legislature. I will not dispute it. I will only observe that the Congress did not think fit so to vest it."[41] An appeal by St. Clair to the attorney general produced an ambiguous decision which supported the governor's position.[42] However, President Jefferson, Secretary of State Madison, and the territorial legislature disagreed. The legislature even refused to provide in law for counties created by St. Clair's dictates.[43] The controversy over county-making seemed to have been dropped after this, though anti-St. Clair feelings continued to grow.[44] Later in 1802, St. Clair acquiesced to the legislature, having lost substantial political support in the battle.[45]

The Ordinance also specified that counties be erected in those parts where Indian titles had been extinguished, a noble policy that was not faithfully heeded. As far back as the Proclamation of 1763, colonial and territorial boundaries had been designed to respect Indian possessions.[46] Even Benjamin Franklin and the Treaty of 1783 sought to protect against encroachments upon Indian lands.[47] Nevertheless, violations of Indian lands continued well into the period of organized settlement in the territory. For example, the Indiana State Senate, apparently concerned over such violations, adopted a resolution in its 1826–27 session recommending that the Committee on the Judiciary "enquire into our constitutional jurisdiction over persons and property, upon lands occupied by Indians, within our territorial limits; and into the expediency of . . . designing county boundaries upon said lands. . . ."[48] In subsequent years, several counties were established in Indiana which violated the territorial rights of the Indians and which acted upon them "like the tightening of a vise."[49]

Section eight of the Ordinance was intended to enumerate the powers necessary for the organization and successful development of the Northwest Territory: in this case, the creation of local governments and the adoption of uniform civil and criminal codes. However, the provisions of this section caused a great controversy between the governor and legislature, primarily over the extent of legislative authority. The governor's preoccupation with executive power resulted in a gradual loss of control over local government, thereby allowing local officials to define the powers needed to govern and to address the needs of settlers in the devoloping West.

DGV

[SECTION 9]

So soon as there shall be five thousand free male inhabitants of full age in the district upon giving proof thereof to

the governor, they shall receive authority with time and
place to elect representatives from their counties or townships to represent them in the general assembly, provided
that for every five hundred free male inhabitants there
shall be one representative and so on progressively with
the number of free male inhabitants shall the right of representation encrease until the number of representatives
shall amount to twenty five after which the number and
proportion of representatives shall be regulated by the
legislature; provided that no person be eligible or qualified
to act as a representative unless he shall have been a citizen of one of the United States three years and be a resident in the district or unless he shall have resided in the
district three years and in either case shall likewise hold in
his own right in fee simple two hundred acres of land
within the same; provided also that a freehold in fifty
acres of land in the district having been a citizen of one of
the states and being resident in the district; or the like
freehold and two years residence in the district shall be
necessary to qualify a man as an elector of a representative

When the free[50] male population, aged twenty-one
and older, reached 5,000, the territory could advance to the
second, or semi-representative, stage of government.[51]
Hereafter, an elective legislature would share power with
officers appointed from outside. As a first step in the transition to partial self-government, the governor would au-
thorize qualified adult males to elect representatives to the
general assembly from their localities. Apportionment of
the representatives was left to the governor.

Initially, the number of representatives was imposed
by Congress at a fixed ratio of one representative for every
five hundred free adult male inhabitants. This formula
would remain in force until the number of representatives
reached twenty-five, after which the general assembly
would assume responsibility for regulating the number
and apportionment of representatives.[52]

Prospective representatives had to meet property and
residence qualifications. To qualify for election to the lower

house a man had to be the owner of at least two hundred acres of land in the district. In addition he had to be a citizen of one of the states for three years and a resident of the district, or, if an alien, he must have lived in the district for three years.[53] These restrictive qualifications for voting and officeholding, seemingly out of place in a "democratic" ordinance, were in fact common in nearly all the older states. At the time the Ordinance was adopted, only Vermont granted manhood suffrage.[54]

Voters were also subject to property and residence qualifications. Besides being a free adult male, the requirements were ownership of at least fifty acres of land in the district, citizenship in one of the states, and residence in the district; or, for non-citizens, the ownership of fifty acres of land in the district and two years' residence.[55]

AFJ

[SECTION 10]

The representatives thus elected shall serve for the term of two years and in case of the death of a representative or removal from office, the governor shall issue a writ to the county or township for which he was a member, to elect another in his stead to serve for the residue of the term

This section specified that representatives were to serve two-year terms. In the event of a representative's death, resignation, or removal from office, the governor was to call a special election in the district in order to fill the vacancy. The man elected would serve out the remainder of the two-year term.

AFJ

[SECTION 11]

The general assembly or legislature shall consist of the governor, legislative council and a house of representatives. The legislative council shall consist of five members to continue in Office five years unless sooner removed by Congress any three of whom to be a quorum and the members of the council shall be nominated and appointed in the following manner, to wit; as soon as representatives shall be elected the governor shall appoint a time & place for them to meet together, and when met they shall nominate ten persons residents in the district and each possessed of a freehold in five hundred acres of Land and return their names to Congress; five of whom Congress shall appoint & commission to serve as aforesaid; and whenever a vacancy shall happen in the council by death or removal from office, the house of Representatives shall nominate two persons qualified as aforesaid, for each vacancy, and return their names to Congress; one of whom Congress shall appoint and commission for the residue of the term; and every five years, four Months at least before the expiration of the time of service of the Members of Council, the said house shall nominate ten persons qualified as aforesaid, and return their names to Congress, five of whom Congress shall appoint and commission to serve as Members of the Council five years, unless sooner removed. And the Governor, legislative Council, and house of Representatives, shall have authority to make laws in all cases for the good government of the district, not repugnant to the principles and Articles in this Ordinance established and declared. And all bills having passed by a majority in the house, and by a Majority in the Council, shall be referred to the Governor for his assent; but no bill or legislative Act whatever, shall be of any force without his assent. The Governor shall have power to convene, prorogue and dissolve the General Assembly, when in his opinion it shall be expedient—

The second stage of territorial government resembled closely the pattern of royal colonial government before the American Revolution. The elected house of representatives corresponded to the lower house in the colonial assemblies. The appointed legislative council formed an upper house similar to the colonial governor's council. Together with the governor these two bodies formed the general assembly.

The legislative council was elected by a procedure in which both voters and the national government shared.

The five members of the council would be chosen at large by Congress from among ten men nominated by the territorial house of representatives.[56] Nominees had to be residents of the district and own five hundred acres of land or more. Councilors would serve five-year terms (reduced to four in 1809), unless sooner removed. Any three constituted a quorum for purposes of business. In the event of a vacancy in the council, the territorial house was to submit two names to Congress, one of whom would be picked to complete the term. The process of nomination and appointment of councilors was to be repeated every five years until statehood.[57]

During the second stage of government the general assembly was empowered to legislate for the district on all local matters. It could not make laws inconsistent with the Articles of Confederation,[58] the acts of the national Congress, the various state land cessions, or other covenants.

The Ordinance gave the appointed governor broad powers, thereby assuring Congress of control over representative government in the territories. The governor's final authority rested on two grants of power: first, an absolute veto over all legislation passed by the assembly, and, second, power to convene, prorogue (terminate), or dissolve the general assembly whenever he thought it necessary.

AFJ

[SECTION 12]

The Governor, Judges, legislative Council, Secretary, and such other Officers as Congress shall appoint in the district, shall take an Oath or Affirmation of fidelity, and of Office, the Governor before the President of Congress, and all other Office[r]s before the Governor. As soon as a legislature shall be formed in the district, the Council and house assembled in one room, shall have authority by joint ballot to elect a Delegate to Congress, who shall have a seat in Congress, with a right of debating, but not of voting, during this temporary Government.

Following English law, practiced in the colonies and generally incorporated in state constitutions after 1776, the Ordinance directed officials to take two oaths or affirmations. The first required the office holder to swear allegiance or "fidelity" to the United States and its laws. The second, an oath or an affirmation of office, obliged the official to faithfully execute the duties of the position. A solemn "affirmation" provided an option for those who for conscience sake could not take an oath, as for example the Quakers, who scorned authority and refused to serve in armies, pay taxes, or take oaths. Whereas the oath-taker might conclude an oath by repeating the words "so help me God," the affirmer might close with the phrase "under the pains and penalties of perjury."[59]

The Ordinance made provision, as had Jefferson's plan of 1784, for a delegate in Congress. This action occurred during the second stage of the territory, that is, with the formation of a territorial legislature. The delegate was to be chosen at a joint meeting of the territorial council and its house of representatives. The territorial house organized on September 23, 1799, and on October 3, 1799, it elected William Henry Harrison over Arthur St. Clair, Jr., as its congressional delegate. Harrison made his appearance in Congress at Philadelphia in December 1799 and resigned in March 1800 to become governor of the newly created Indiana Territory. Harrison was only the second territorial representative sent to Congress. The first territorial delegate to Congress was Dr. James White, representing the Territory Southwest of the River Ohio. White was elected in 1794 and served until 1796, when the territory became the state of Tennessee.

Because the Ordinance did not specify privileges and duties beyond those of debating and of not voting, precedents and traditions were set by decisions in Congress about the status of a delegate and by the initiatives of the delegates themselves. Questions arose as to whether the delegate should sit in both the Senate and the House of Representatives since he was elected to "Congress" in the

Ordinance. Should he sit only in the Senate since he was elected in the manner of senators? Was it necessary for him to take an oath since he would not be a voting member? What of mailing privileges and salary? Congress resolved the seating issue by putting the delegate in the House of Representatives. Congress also granted the delegate pay and postal allowances equal to those of congressmen. Harrison established the precedent of taking an oath, and he also, according to Jo Tice Bloom, set the tone for an activist role in the House by chairing a select committee. Standing committees were generally off-limits to the early delegates. The delegates' most important tasks were attending to territorial matters, securing beneficial legislation, presenting petitions, and pushing for an enabling act for statehood for the territory. The representation of territories by delegates to Congress continued until 1959.[60]

RMT

[SECTION 13]

And for extending the fundamental principles of Civil and religious liberty, which form the basis whereon these Republics, their laws and constitutions are erected; to fix and establish those principles as the basis of all laws, constitutions and governments, which forever hereafter shall be formed in the said territory;—to provide also for the establishment of States, and permanent government therein, and for their admission to a share in the federal Councils on an equal footing with the original States, at as early periods as may be consistent with the general interest—

Section thirteen of the Northwest Ordinance is a transitional paragraph which introduces the Articles of Compact between the government of the United States and the people of the Northwest Territory. It resembles the preamble of the U.S. Constitution in that it explains the goals of the framers in setting forth these guidelines and guarantees. The original form of section thirteen appeared in a report presented to Congress on March 1, 1784, and approved on April 23 of that year. It was incorporated in successive drafts of the Ordinance and ultimately in the final document.[61]

The provisions of section thirteen recognize certain basic principles of government that the people of the original states had insisted on as vital during their revolutionary struggle. Reliable sources indicate that its authors drew from "the previous ordinances, the motions of Grayson, the Code of Massachusetts, and perhaps the constitutions or laws of other states."[62] Settlers moving westward carried with them these same ideals, and urged that they be written into a framework of government for the new territory. Several main phrases are worthy of note:

the fundamental principles of Civil and religious liberty

This is a reference to certain cherished guarantees drawn both from English heritage and from colonial experience. Principles of civil liberty included such "rights of Englishmen" as the right to a writ of habeas corpus, right to trial by jury, and a right to taxation only by consent of the governed. Drawn originally from the Magna Carta, these guarantees had been exacted repeatedly from the British government and then incorporated in the new frameworks of government in America after independence. Reference to religious liberty was of relatively more recent origin. This concept had developed in the colonies in the seventeenth and eighteenth centuries and had become of increasing importance as peoples of many backgrounds came to settle in America. It was incorporated in this document at the suggestion of Thomas Jefferson.

to fix and establish those principles as the basis of all laws, constitutions and governments, which forever hereafter shall be formed in the said territory

This passage provides a guarantee of the permanence of the rights and protections with which the settlers were concerned. They wanted assurances not only to serve their immediate needs, but for the future. Correspondence received in Philadelphia in the spring of 1786 indicated that these concerns were supported by those states whose cessions had made creation of the territory possible.[63]

> To provide also for the establishment of States, and permanent government therein, and for their admission to a share in the federal Councils on an equal footing with the original States, at as early periods as may be consistent with the general interest

This section was written in response to concerns that the territories be allowed to develop into full-fledged states without delay. Some negotiators would have preferred to keep the western lands in a subservient status indefinitely, but opposition to such an arrangement came from those who were concerned with binding the region to the United States as quickly and firmly as possible in order to avoid possible interference from Britain or Spain. Speculators interested in the rapid development of the territory also believed a strong government essential.[64] Concerns of men like Elbridge Gerry that the regions west of the Appalachians would someday outrank the original states in population and power could not withstand such compelling arguments. Several draft proposals of the Ordinance of 1787 emphasized the principle of equality, including the Financier's Plan of June 1783 and Jefferson's Plan of 1784.[65]

Having completed these introductory remarks, the authors of the Ordinance of 1787 then proceeded to an enumeration of the guarantees.

RSS

[SECTION 14]

It is hereby Ordained and declared by the authority aforesaid, That the following Articles shall be considered as Articles of compact between the Original States and the

People and States in the said territory, and forever remain
unalterable, unless by common consent, to wit,

One of the main areas of disagreement between the
American colonies and the British government, prior to the
American Revolution, concerned the nature of rights
granted colonists by colonial charters. Americans firmly
believed they had all the rights of Englishmen and that
their charters provided a written foundation for basic free-
doms. In the view of the British government all rights of
colonists and colonial charters were subject to the over-
riding power of the King and Parliament. Thomas Jefferson
in the Declaration of Independence referred to this conflict
when he condemned King George III "for taking away our
charters, abolishing our most valuable laws, and altering
fundamentally the forms of our governments."

Americans, who had just completed a long and bloody
war in defense of what they believed to be inalienable
rights, were not willing to colonize the Northwest Territory
without assurance that their rights would not be sacrificed.
Section fourteen of the Ordinance of 1787 provided that
assurance. It created a compact, the most solemn agreement known to eighteenth-century political science. By the
terms of the compact, rights granted colonists of the Northwest Territory by the six articles of the Ordinance would
"forever remain unalterable, unless by common consent...." Unlike the colonial policy of Great Britain, the
colonial policy of the United States was to be built upon
recognition of inalienable rights. Colonists were to be
granted all the legal and political rights enjoyed by citizens
of the mother country. In drafting section fourteen of the
Ordinance of 1787, Congress remained true to the ideals
expressed in the Declaration of Independence.

HCK

ARTICLE THE FIRST

No person demeaning himself in a peaceable and orderly
manner shall ever be molested on account of his mode of
worship or religious sentiments in the said territory—

The first of the "Articles of Compact" reaffirms a principle already widely accepted in the American popular mind by 1787—namely, the right of anyone to practice religion freely and without fear of interference. In granting religious liberty as the premier right for the inhabitants of the Northwest Territory, the Ordinance thus took its place as "one of the fundamental documents in the history of American religious freedom."[66]

By the time of the Ordinance's adoption, that history was already a long and heroic one. Fortunately, as William Warren Sweet observed a half-century ago, the American colonial environment was a fertile one for the cultivation of religious freedom. The British colonial policy was characterized by a sort of "religious laissez faire," and it permitted the influx of a variety of spiritual and ethnic groups from western Europe who came to the English colonies seeking escape from religious intolerance or persecution. Such minorities—Mennonites, Dunkers, Schwenkfelders, Welsh Baptists, and others—quite naturally and fervently advocated religious liberty. Furthermore, the American colonies contained an extraordinary number of unchurched folk. They constituted a "large body of religiously indifferent people" who became, in Sweet's view, "an important element in the growth of the spirit of religious tolerance."[67]

Even more crucial in the colonial development of religious liberty were the courageous actions of dedicated individuals and groups. While the story of Roger Williams is clearly the most celebrated instance, countless Quakers, Baptists, and Separatists from Massachusetts to Maryland struck blows for the cause of the unshackled mind.[68] Then, as the colonies moved into the volatile eighteenth century, European Enlightenment thought found a comfortable seedbed in colonial intellectual soil. American thinkers, foremost among them the young Thomas Jefferson, discovered in John Locke and the French *philosophes*, and in the doctrine of natural rights, a framework for their growing belief in freedom of religion. During the last three decades of the century, Americans incorporated that doctrine into a host of memorials, legislative acts, and constitutions.[69] Undoubtedly, the classic example is that of Virginia.

According to Anson Phelps Stokes, the Virginia struggle for liberty of conscience "influenced the American theories of Church-State separation and religious freedom more than any other historical factor."[70] Although Baptists took the lead in championing the cause, memorializing the Virginia House of Burgesses as early as 1772 for a recognition of rights of conscience, the major actors in the fight were, of course, Thomas Jefferson and James Madison.

The concept of freedom of religion lay at the very core of Jefferson's philosophy. In 1776, when authoring a series of drafts for a state constitution, Jefferson included in each the provision that "all persons shall have full and free liberty of religious opinion."[71] The famous "Bill for Establishing Religious Freedom," however, was Jefferson's outstanding contribution to the battle for freedom of the mind. First prepared in 1777, but not declared law until January 1786, the bill proclaimed that "Almightly God hath created the mind free" and that, therefore, "all men shall be free to profess, and by argument to maintain, their opinions, in matters of religion. . . ."[72]

It was James Madison, not Jefferson, who finally got the religious liberty bill through the Virginia legislature, but not before he himself had devoted years of hard work in pursuit of that goal. In his first major public act, as a youthful member of the House of Burgesses in 1776, he objected to an early draft of a declaration of rights written by George Mason because it called for "the fullest *tolerance* in the Exercise of Religion," rather than a more liberal policy of "*full* and *free* exercise of Religion," which Madison proposed in a subsequent amendment.[73] A decade later, when the Virginia legislature drafted a General Assessment Bill which would levy a tax for the support of religion, Madison wrote and circulated "A Memorial and Remonstrance" which attacked the bill. Considered his most important public paper dealing with freedom of religion, this petition declared that the religion "of every man must be left to the conviction and conscience of every man; and it is the right of every man to exercise it as these may dictate."[74]

By 1787, then, the foundations had been firmly laid for legal enactments of the principle of religious freedom. The most immediate precedents for this article of the Ordinance, however, appear to be the constitutions and bills of rights of the original states, all of which had been influenced by the fruitful heritage of the struggle for religious freedom.[75] Even the article's language derived from these documents, as well as from other legal works. The word "molested," for example, was the standard term used in colonial and early national writings when referring to the person's right to non-interference in matters of religious beliefs and practices. William Penn's "Great Law" contained the word, as did the religious freedom provisions of numerous treaties and even Jefferson's renowned "Bill for Establishing Religious Freedom."[76]

It was also customary, given the prevailing view of elitist decision-makers toward the frontiersmen—whom they perceived as a crude, lawless, discontented, adventuresome lot—to include a phrase calling for "peaceable and orderly" behavior. Writing to George Washington only two days after the Ordinance's passage, Richard Henry Lee expressed this aristocratic view: "it seemed necessary, for the security of the property among uninformed, and perhaps licentious people as the greater part of those who go there are, that a strong toned government should exist...."[77] Apparently, the enactors of the Northwest Ordinance not only intended for religion in the new territory to be free, but also that it serve as a means for promoting social order.

LAH

ARTICLE THE SECOND

The Inhabitants of the said territory shall always be entitled to the benefits of the writ of habeas corpus, and of the trial by Jury; of a proportionate representation of the people in the legislature, and of judicial proceedings according to the course of the common law; all Persons shall be bailable unless for capital offences, where the proof shall be evident, or the presumption great; all fines shall be moderate, and no cruel or unusual punishments shall be inflicted; no man shall be deprived of his liberty or property but by the judgment of his Peers, or the law of the land; and should the public exigencies make it necessary for the common preservation to take any persons property, or to demand his particular services, full compensation shall be made for the same;—and in the just preservation of rights and property it is understood and declared, that no law ought ever to be made, or have force in the said territory, that shall in any manner whatever interfere with, or affect private contracts or engagements, bona fide and without fraud previously formed

In the Declaration of Independence Thomas Jefferson, writing for the American colonies, declared that governments are created to secure "unalienable rights." Following the American Revolution these rights were defined at a national level in two great documents: the Northwest Ordinance of 1787 and the United States Constitution together with its Bill of Rights. Article Two of the Ordinance contains many of the limitations on government power necessary to secure these rights. These limitations were later included in the Constitution and Bill of Rights. Article Two deals primarily with the rights belonging to a person accused of a crime.

By far the most important single right contained in the article is the entitlement to writs of habeas corpus, a right later included in Article One, section nine, of the Constitution. Habeas corpus safeguards all other rights by permitting any prisoner or friend of a prisoner to go to a judge and obtain an order that the prisoner be produced together with an explanation of the cause of detention. If the judge determines the prisoner's rights have been violated and the detention is illegal, the prisoner is set free. It is the ability of a prisoner to require his detention be reviewed by an independent judge that permits courts to insure other rights are not violated.

Other rights afforded by Article Two to those accused of crimes and later included in the United States Constitution are these: (1) the right to bail in noncapital cases (Eighth Amendment); (2) the right to trial by jury (Sixth Amendment); (3) the right to be safe from cruel or unusual punishment (Eighth Amendment); and (4) the right to judicial proceedings according to the course of the common law ("due process of law," Fifth Amendment).

In addition to rights given those accused of crimes, Article Two also declared other rights which later found acceptance in the United States Constitution. They are (1) the right of a proportionate representation of the people in the legislature (Article One, section two; Article Four, section four); (2) the right to be compensated for property or services of an individual that are taken for public use (Fifth Amendment); and (3) the right to make private contracts which the government may not interfere with (Article One, section ten).

The Northwest Ordinance of 1787 and the American Constitution were both natural products of the Declaration of Independence. Each document sought to define those unalienable rights referred to by Thomas Jefferson. It is not extraordinary that the rights expressed in both are similar. They stand together as two of the first and greatest expressions of the natural rights of citizens in a free nation.

HCK

ARTICLE THE THIRD

Religion, Morality and knowledge being necessary to good government and the happiness of mankind, Schools and the means of education shall forever be encouraged. The utmost good faith shall always be observed towards the Indians; their lands and property shall never be taken from them without their consent; and in their property, rights and liberty, they never shall be invaded or disturbed, unless in just and lawful wars authorised by Congress; but laws founded in justice and humanity shall from time to time be made, for preventing wrongs being done to them, and for preserving peace and friendship with them—

The brief reference to the Indians in the third article of the Northwest Ordinance has seemed to many commentators to be at best ironic and at worst hypocritical. After all, the lands that the Ordinance was designed to organize politically were still inhabited by Indians who showed no inclination to move. If "the utmost good faith" was indeed to be exercised toward the native people, if their property was not to be taken without their consent, then the Ordinance and its predecessors in 1784 and 1785 would seem to have been efforts in wishful thinking. Since the Revolution the Indians had made only minor and reluctant concessions in the Northwest, and by the date of the Ordinance their resistance to any further grants of land had stiffened.

In fact the cryptic policy statement of the Ordinance might have been ironic (very little that white men said or did concerning Indians was not), but it was neither hypocritical nor unrealistic. It rested on long colonial experience of relations with the tribes that was in the course of clarification in these early years of independence. From the very beginning colonial authorities had assumed that European society would displace the Indians in America. There was a minimal hope (and at least some effort to bring it to fruition) that individual natives would be incorporated into the white man's world, but in no case was it assumed that Indian society would remain intact and in possession of any substantial segment of the continent. Hence there was not, in the white man's thinking, any incompatibility between the "utmost good faith" and the displacement of the native population.

But this expectation for the future of the continent did not mean that the native people could be dispossessed at will. The Indians may not have had a right to property in

America in the same sense that the European governments and settlers were to claim that right, that is in the sense of political sovereignty and in fee-simple ownership, but it was plain to the earliest colonizers that they did have a certain right to the soil. Often enough this was simply a concession to reality; the tribes could defend their claims to ancestral lands. But in time it came to be a legally accepted principle that the Indians possessed a right to the soil, a usufruct that could be liquidated only with consent or by conquest in a just war. The principle rested on the belief that the Indians were a "savage" people living at a pre-civil stage that precluded full property rights. Thus in the seventeenth and eighteenth centuries imperial authorities and, after 1776, agents of the new nation expended much effort in formal dealings with the native people designed to bring them into alliance or to open lands for white settlement. These formal negotiations were often marred by manipulation or outright fraud, in itself a backhanded concession that Indian lands could not be obtained without the consent of the tribes. The principle was plainly implied in both Jefferson's Ordinance of 1784 and in the Land Ordinance of 1785 and became the basis for the Indian policy after the establishment of the new government in 1789.

Although the government may have recognized the Indians' formal right of possession, land-hungry settlers refused steadfastly to be inconvenienced by such legal niceties. After the Peace of Paris in 1763 the British authorities had attempted to control the movement of settlers into the West but with limited success. In the years after the Revolution, the Confederation government assumed the same obligation with no less difficulty. Often in the Confederation period the frontiersmen were seen as the villains of the drama. Although the government intended ultimately that the western territories should be occupied by white men, it found itself increasingly in the role of mediator between the tribes and the settlers. Turmoil on the frontier or open war with the Indians would cost a great deal of money, a commodity in shortage in the 1780s.

Troops had to be raised and supported, fortifications built, and expeditions against the tribes led across the Ohio. The government preferred an orderly and less expensive transition from native to settler control. Hence the insistence in the ordinances of the 1780s on the consent of the native people in the process.

The reference in the Northwest Ordinance to "just and lawful wars" against the Indians evoked memories of the War for Independence. In that struggle most of the tribes had supported Britain. When the British made peace, they abandoned the tribes to the mercies of the new nation. The Americans, thinking more of the forms than the reality, for they had never in fact defeated the warriors north of the Ohio, attempted to treat the Indians as a conquered people. At three treaties, Fort Stanwix, Fort McIntosh, and at the mouth of the Miami, between 1784 and 1786 they demanded submission and large territorial cessions from the northwestern tribes. But by 1787 this policy had plainly run its course. The Indians had not been subjugated, and the Confederation could not muster the resources to conquer them. Ultimately conquest would prove necessary, but for the time being conciliation seemed the more practical course.

The last clause in Article Three announced the beginnings of a philanthropic policy toward the native people. Beginning with the Intercourse Act of 1790, the federal government initiated a policy which it hoped would keep peace on the frontier and prepare the native people for the transition to "civility." This was the ultimate meaning of "justice and humanity." As Henry Knox, Washington's secretary of war, was to say more than once, the United States must pursue a policy toward the native people that will gain the "approbation of the dispassionate and enlightened part of mankind." Thus for its own reasons the new nation felt a deep obligation toward the Indians, but it was not an obligation that took into consideration the Indians' view of their interests. Nor was it a sense of obligation that would long delay the settlement of the Northwest Territory.

BWS

ARTICLE THE FOURTH

The said territory, and the States which may be formed therein, shall forever remain a part of this Confederacy of the United States of America, subject to the Articles of Confederation, and to such alterations therein as shall be constitutionally made; and to all the Acts and Ordinances of the United States in Congress Assembled, conformable thereto. The Inhabitants and Settlers in the said territory, shall be subject to pay a part of the federal debts contracted or to be contracted, and a proportional part of the expences of Government, to be apportioned on them by Congress, according to the same common rule and measure by which apportionments thereof shall be made on the other States; and the taxes for paying their proportion, shall be laid and levied by the authority and direction of the legislatures of the district or districts or new States, as in the original states, within the time agreed upon by the United States in Congress Assembled. The Legislatures of those districts, or new States, shall never interfere with the primary disposal of the Soil by the United States in Congress Assembled, nor with any regulations Congress may find necessary for securing the title in such soil to the bona fide purchasers. No tax shall be imposed on lands the property of the United States; and in no case shall non Resident proprietors be taxed higher than Residents. The navigable Waters leading into the Mississippi and St. Lawrence, and carrying places between the same shall be common highways, and forever free, as well to the Inhabitants of the said territory, as to the Citizens of the United States, and those of any other States that may be admitted into the Confederacy, without any tax, impost or duty therefor—

When called upon to fit their policies toward the trans-Appalachian West into a larger context, members of the

Confederation Congress often made use of the terms "union" and "empire." The first term reflected a desire to link western lands and settlers permanently within the Confederation; the second term suggested an interest in earlier models of colonial development and in possible competition of Britain or Spain for western allegiances.[78]

No aspect of this competition was more immediate than the troubled negotiations with Spain over reopening the Mississippi River at the Spanish-ruled port of New Orleans. Complaints of western settlers and rumors of a foreign-supported "Spanish conspiracy" had combined with debate over the controversial Jay-Gardoqui trade treaty of 1786 to alarm more than one congressman and to contribute to the reaffirmation of union that opens Article Four.

The idea of union was often linked in congressional discourse to the questions of interstate and international trade. In some cases the linkage reflected such immediate problems as those posed by the Spanish; in others it reflected the more general belief that no central government could function effectively unless it had the power to regulate both domestic and foreign trade. In the largest sense trade thus became a bond of union that could reconcile the interests of citizens and states by giving them common economic ties and associations. Given the lack of internal improvements in the unsettled West, most trade would necessarily move to the rivers and portages that Congress sought to free from commercial restriction in Article Four.

Such affirmations of union were closely tied to the complicated problems of government finance that existed in the 1780s. Under the Articles of Confederation, Congress had not been given the power to lay and collect taxes—a restriction that arose partly from memories of pre-Revolutionary abuses of taxation by the British and partly out of respect for the sovereignty of the thirteen states that composed the Confederation.

Instead, Congress had been given four other means of

dealing with the "power of the purse." First, it could borrow money, at home or abroad, issuing interest-bearing loan office certificates (which were, in effect, bonds). Second, it could print paper money and a variety of other paper obligations that were secured by Congress's promise of future redemption. Third, it could levy requisitions upon the thirteen states, asking them each to bear a portion of the costs of government and/or the debts, interest, and obligations that already existed. Finally, Congress could offer for sale the public lands granted to it by the Treaty of Paris of 1783 and by various land claim cessions of the 1780s.

None of these four approaches had proved totally satisfactory. Borrowing had produced a large national debt whose interest payments proved a major burden after the War for Independence. Paper money had been issued in such quantities that some critics alleged its later issues were "not worth a Continental." Requisitions had often been ignored by state governments or absorbed into complicated schemes by which the states sought to manage their own debt burdens. And land sales had been delayed both by rival state claims and by Indian hostility to surveyors who were attempting to implement the Land Ordinance of 1785.

Despite these problems, Article Four suggests that the western country still offered some potential relief for the financially strapped government. In the long run, as new states emerged and joined the Union, each could be asked to comply with the financial requisitions (apportioned by population or taxable wealth) that were already the responsibility of the existing thirteen states. In the short run, the West continued to offer land that could be sold either to actual settlers or to land speculators (who often remained in the East or in Europe hoping for the value of their purchases to increase). Two years before, in the Land Ordinance of 1785, Congress had first sought to survey and sell the lands north and west of the Ohio River. Now Article Four reaffirmed the title of Congress to those potentially valuable lands and carefully limited the power of new western territories and states either to claim unsold land, to tax settlers and speculators, or to challenge congressional authority as land sales proceeded.

Congress also took implicit notice in Article Four of an important shift in the manner by which western land might be sold. Under the earlier 1785 ordinance it had been assumed that land would be offered in fairly small tracts, no larger than a township at a time. By 1787 Congress was actively considering an alternative method of sale: granting the land to large private companies that could make payments in government securities, thus reducing the national debt. The Ohio Company, a group of investors centered in New England, were actively seeking a large tract of land along the Ohio and Muskingum rivers west of the Seven Ranges (in the far southeastern corner of modern Ohio). Offering immediate payment, the investors were insistent that Congress enact an ordinance that would both protect land titles and attract settlers from the New England (or eastern) states. It is thus generally accepted that members of the Ohio Company were consulted about the terms of public land and finance policy found in Article Four.

GCG

ARTICLE THE FIFTH

There shall be formed in the said territory, not less than three nor more than five States; and the boundaries of the States, as soon as Virginia shall alter her act of Cession and consent to the same, shall become fixed and established as follows, to wit: The Western State in the said territory, shall be bounded by the Mississippi, the Ohio and Wabash Rivers; a direct line drawn from the Wabash and post Vincents due North to the territorial line between the United States and Canada, and by the said territorial line to the lake of the Woods and Mississippi. The middle State shall be bounded by the said direct line, the Wabash from post Vincents to the Ohio; by the Ohio, by a direct line drawn due North from the mouth of the great Miami to the said territorial line, and by the said territorial line.—The eastern State shall be bounded by the last mentioned direct line, the Ohio, Pennsylvania, and the said territorial line; provided however, and it is further understood and declared, that the boundaries of these three States, shall be subject so far to be altered, that if Congress shall hereafter find it expedient, they shall have authority to form one or two States in that part of the said territory which lies north of an east and west line drawn through the southerly bend or extreme of lake Michigan: and whenever any of the said States shall have sixty thousand free Inhabitants therein, such State shall be admitted by its Delegates into the Congress[79] of the United States, on an equal footing with the original States, in all respects whatever; and shall be at liberty to form a permanent Constitution and State Government; provided the Constitution and Government so to be formed, shall be Republican, and in conformity to the principles contained in these Articles; and so far as it can be consistent with the general interest of the Confederacy, such admission shall be allowed at an earlier period, and when there may be a less number of free Inhabitants in the State than sixty thousand.

By the time the Northwest Ordinance was adopted, there had already been considerable debate over how the western territory should be divided into states for eventual admission into the Union. In Virginia's March 1, 1784, Act of Cession relinquishing her western land claims, the stipulation was made that "the Territory so ceded shall be laid out and formed into States containing a suitable extent of Territory not less than one hundred nor more than one hundred and fifty miles square or as near thereto as circumstances will admit...."[80] On the same day the Virginia cession was executed, a congressional committee chaired by Thomas Jefferson submitted a plan for the temporary government of the western lands. Both the "Jefferson plan" and the somewhat modified ordinance that was actually adopted on April 23, 1784, provided for a relatively large number of northwestern states, their boundaries based on latitudinal and longitudinal lines rather than natural features.[81]

There was not, however, universal agreement with this scheme (and, indeed, the 1784 ordinance was never really operative). James Monroe, in particular, felt that the number of states to be formed out of the northwestern territory should be reduced—partially to insure the dominance of the eastern states and partially to make it easier for the western states to achieve the requisite population to become self-governing.[82] This point of view prevailed during the drafting of the Northwest Ordinance, and provision was thus made for a minimum of three and a maximum of five new states.[83] But Virginia's Act of Cession, limiting states to be created out of her ceded territory to 150 miles square, remained an obstacle. Virginia was therefore requested to revise her Act of Cession, and the language of Article Five anticipates that revision. Virginia complied in an act of December 30, 1788.[84]

Two of the nation's principal waterways—the Ohio and Mississippi rivers—defined the southern and western boundaries of the Northwest Territory. (The land west of the Mississippi was then under Spanish control; the area south of the Ohio had not yet been ceded to Congress.) The territory's eastern boundary was the western border of Pennsylvania and the northern limit was the international border separating the United States and Canada. The article also delineated the boundaries separating the three states that were definitely to be formed from the territory. The Wabash River and a line running north from "post Vincents" (present Vincennes, Indiana) separated the "western" and "middle" states (eventually, Illinois and Indiana). The "middle" and "eastern" states (Indiana and Ohio) were separated by a line drawn due north from the mouth of the Great Miami River. Provision was also made for the possible creation of two additional states (which became Michigan and Wisconsin) to be formed north of an east-west line drawn through the southern tip of Lake

Michigan. This rather arbitrary boundary was somewhat altered in the enabling acts that admitted the states of the Northwest Territory into the federal Union; it did not, in fact, end up being the actual border between Michigan-Ohio, Michigan-Indiana, or Illinois-Wisconsin.[85] (See Map 4.)

There was debate as well over the population that should be required for the new states to be admitted to the Union. The ordinance of April 23, 1784, required that a prospective state should have "of free inhabitants, as many as shall then be in any one [of] the least numerous of the thirteen original states."[86] During the committee discussions leading toward the Northwest Ordinance, it was proposed that the population requirement for admission to the Union be "raised to one thirteenth of the whole population of the original States"—a figure that would have been, as of 1780, approximately 200,000.[87] This proposal was rejected, and a requirement of 60,000 free inhabitants was substituted. The final clause of Article Five, however, provided that the 60,000 requirement could be waived should the Congress, in a particular instance, determine such action to be "consistent with the general interest" of the nation.[88]

One of the most important provisions in the Ordinance is the injunction in Article Five that the new states created out of the Northwest Territory were to be admitted to the Union "on an equal footing with the original States, in all respects whatever." This principle, subsequently extended to each new state that entered the Union, precluded a permanent colonial status for any of the territory west of the original coastal states. The article also insisted that the constitutions and governments of the new northwestern states were to be republican in form (that is, representative democracies) and conform to the other provisions of the Ordinance.

RMB & SAM

ARTICLE THE SIXTH

There shall be neither Slavery nor involuntary Servitude in the said territory otherwise than in the punishment of crimes, whereof the Party shall have been duly convicted: Provided always that any Person escaping into the same, from whom labor or service is lawfully claimed in any one of the original States, such fugitive may be lawfully reclaimed and conveyed to the person claiming his or her labor or service as aforesaid—

Before the adoption of Article Six there had been efforts to exclude slavery from the lands in the West. The most important was a proposal by the committee that framed the Ordinance of 1784. It declared that after 1800 there should be "neither slavery nor involuntary servitude" in any of the new states created out of western lands, and was narrowly defeated in the Congress. All of the members from states north of the Mason-Dixon line, who were present at the time of the vote, voted in favor; all those from south of the line, except Thomas Jefferson of Virginia, voted against.[89]

While the Ordinance of 1787 was under consideration, Nathan Dane, a member from Massachusetts, moved a sixth "article of compact," banning slavery from the Northwest Territory. Later Rufus King proposed the addition of the clause for the return of fugitive slaves. The entire Ordinance, including Article Six, was then passed with the assent of all eight states present. A fact, frequently overlooked by historians, is that a majority of the states present were southern states. The eight states present were Georgia, South Carolina, North Carolina, Virginia, Delaware, New Jersey, New York, and Massachusetts. All the members present voted for the Ordinance except Abraham Yates of New York. All of the southern states except Maryland were present. Three New England states and Pennsylvania were not present.[90]

The motives for the framing and adoption of Article Six have been subjects of speculation and conjecture, but little solid contemporary evidence exists to account for them. Especially puzzling is the fact that members from southern states voted against the prohibition of slavery in the Ordinance of 1784, but voted for Article Six of the Ordinance of 1787. An obvious difference between the two, of course, was that the 1784 proposal would have banned slavery in all the new states in the West, while the Ordinance of 1787 applied only to lands north of the Ohio River. By implication lands south of the river remained open to slavery. Some think that Article Six was accepted because prohibition of slavery would deter cultivation of crops (tobacco and indigo) which would compete with those of the older slave states. Others have speculated that southern members of Congress expected that southerners would dominate migration to the Northwest Territory and that agrarian interests, with or without slavery, would lead to a political alliance between the older states of the South and the new western states at the expense of New England.[91] One recent historian (Staughton Lynd) has even theorized that there was a tacit understanding (the "Compromise of 1787") between members of the Constitutional Convention and members of the 1787 Congress to protect slavery in the existing states while excluding it from the lands north of the Ohio.[92]

Whatever the motives and intentions of the framers, Article Six did not end slavery or involuntary servitude in the Northwest Territory. The Ordinance itself guaranteed to the French inhabitants "their laws and customs now in force among them, relative to the descent and conveyance of property." The provisions on suffrage and apportionment of representation referring to "free male inhabitants" suggested the legal existence of slavery. Although there were some differences of opinion as to the effect of Article Six, the usual interpretation by territorial governors and judges was that the article was not intended to be retroactive—that it prohibited introduction of more slaves but did not affect the status of those already in the territory and their descendants. These slaves and their children continued to live in bondage and were sold and bequeathed in wills.[93]

As new settlers moved into Indiana Territory some of them petitioned Congress to modify Article Six so as to permit slaves to be brought into the territory for a limited number of years. Failing in these efforts, the pro-slavery groups succeeded in evading Article Six by a system of slavery thinly disguised as indentured servitude. "An Act concerning the Introduction of Negroes and Mulattoes into This Territory," adopted in 1805 permitted any person owning or purchasing slaves outside the territory to bring them into Indiana and bind them to service. Slaves over fifteen years of age could be required to contract to serve any number of years. If they refused this "voluntary" service they could be taken out of the territory and sold as slaves. Slaves less than fifteen years of age were required to serve until the age of thirty-five if males, thirty-two if females. Children born to slaves after they were brought into the territory were required to serve the master of the parent until the age of thirty if males; twenty-eight if females.[94]

A report of a territorial legislative committee in 1808 characterized the law as "contrary both to the spirit and letter of the Ordinance" and said the "most flagitious abuse" was made of it. Records show that slaves were frequently made to sign contracts for periods of service which would extend beyond their lifetime—sometimes for ninety years. Most contracts called for twenty or forty years of service. Many wealthy and prominent men in the territory, including governors William Henry Harrison and Thomas Posey, held Negroes under the indenture law.[95]

In 1810, after the separation of Indiana and Illinois territories, the indenture law was repealed, but this in no way affected indentures already made. Moreover, despite repeal some Negroes continued to be brought into Indiana and required to sign contracts for long terms of service.

Blacks made up only a tiny fraction of the total population of Indiana Territory, a mere 630 as compared to

23,890 whites according to the census of 1810. Most of them were concentrated near Vincennes in Knox County. From census figures it is impossible to distinguish accurately between persons who were slaves and those held as indentured servants or between indentured servants and free Negroes. In practice there was little difference in the status and treatment of slaves who had been in the territory before 1787 and their descendants and those serving under indentures. Members of both groups continued to be bought and sold and to be bequeathed in wills. Territorial laws borrowed from the slave codes of the South regulated their conduct and provided punishments for offenses different from those accorded free persons. But some police regulations applied to free Negroes as well as slaves and servants.[96]

Delegates opposed to slavery dominated the convention which met in 1816 to write a constitution for the state of Indiana. One article in the finished document provided that there should be an opportunity to amend the constitution every ten years but with the proviso that slavery and involuntary servitude should never be introduced. The Bill of Rights, in language almost identical with Article Six of the Ordinance of 1787 declared: "There shall be neither slavery nor involuntary servitude in this State, otherwise than for the punishment of crimes whereof the party shall have been duly convicted, nor shall any indenture of any negro [sic] or mulatto hereafter made and executed out of the bounds of this State be of any validity within the State."[97]

After the constitution went into effect several freedom suits were instituted in Knox County Court. The case of a woman named Polly was appealed to the Indiana Supreme Court. Because she was the daughter of a slave woman purchased by a French inhabitant before the Ordinance of 1787, the Knox County Court, ignoring the state constitution, held that she was still a slave. Rejecting the argument that the French settlers had vested rights which could not be destroyed by the state constitution, the supreme court reversed the lower court, declaring that "under our present form of government, slavery can have no existence in the State of Indiana."[98]

This decision did not deal with the status of indentured servants, who continued to be held and sometimes sold despite the 1816 constitution. In 1821 the state's highest court again reversed the decision of Knox County Court. In a case brought by a woman who sought release from her indenture the supreme court held that the mere fact that she brought suit was evidence that her servitude was "involuntary" and hence in violation of the state constitution. Although some few masters may have continued to hold blacks in bondage as slaves or indentured servants, questions as to the legality of such bondage had been clearly answered by the Indiana Supreme Court five years after the admission of Indiana to statehood.[99]

ELT

Be it ordained by the Authority aforesaid, that the Resolutions of the 23d of April 1784, relative to the subject of this ordinance be, and the same are hereby repealed and declared null and void.
   Done &c

This final part of the Ordinance gave it legal precedence over the Ordinance of 1784. Though it had legal status prior to the enactment of the Ordinance of 1787, the Ordinance of 1784 had not been accorded serious consideration as a workable model for organizing the western country.

In the official printed copy of the Northwest Ordinance (see the text on the reverse side of the map in the end pocket) the last phrase, "Done &c," is stated in full: "Done by the United States in Congress assembled, the 13th day of July, in the year of our Lord 1787, and of their sovereignty and independence the 12th." The United States, just a little over a week before the Ordinance became law, had celebrated its eleventh year of independence.

Also on this broadside is the signature of Charles Thomson (1729–1824), secretary of the Confederation Congress. Born in Ireland and a Quaker, Thomson began his service as secretary when elected on September 5, 1774, at the First Continental Congress. He stayed in that office for almost fifteen years.

RMT

Map 1:

OLD NORTHWEST REGION, 1783–90

Map 1. *[Wiley Sword,* **President Washington's Indian War: The Struggle for the Old Northwest, 1790–1795** *(Norman, Okla.: University of Oklahoma Press, 1985).]*

UNITED STATES AFTER 1783

Map 2. *[Richard B. Morris and Jeffrey B. Morris, eds.,* **Encyclopedia of American History,** *6th ed. (New York: Harper and Row, 1982).]*

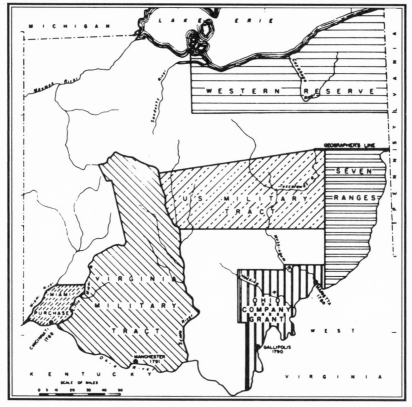

Map 3. *Chief Ohio land divisions, the Geographer's Line, and the earliest settlements.*
[*Beverley W. Bond, Jr.,* **The Foundations of Ohio,** *vol. 1 (Columbus, Ohio Historical Society, 1941).]*

Map 4. *Changes in the southern boundary of Michigan Territory (drawn by George Pence, 1927).*
[*Mrs. Frank J. Sheehan,* **The Northern Boundary of Indiana,** *Indiana Historical Society* **Publications,** *vol. 8, no. 6 (Indianapolis, 1928).]*

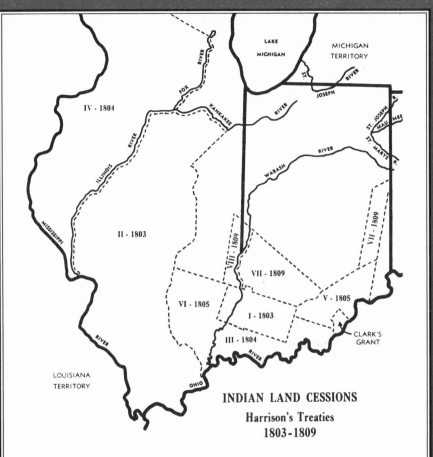

INDIAN LAND CESSIONS

Harrison's Treaties
1803-1809

I. June 7, 1803, at Fort Wayne, with the Delawares, Shawnee, Potawatomi, Miami, Eel Rivers, Wea, Kickapoo, Piankashaw, and Kaskaskia.

II. August 13, 1803, at Vincennes, with the Kaskaskia.

III. August 18 and 27, 1804, at Vincennes, with the Delawares and Piankashaw.

IV. November 3, 1804, at St. Louis, with the Sauk and Foxes.

V. August 21, 1805, at Grouseland, with the Delawares, Potawatomi, Miami, Eel Rivers, and Wea.

VI. December 30, 1805, at Vincennes, with the Piankashaw.

VII. September 30, 1809, at Fort Wayne, with the Delawares, Potawatomi, Miami, Eel Rivers, and Wea.

VIII. December 9, 1809, at Vincennes, with the Kickapoo.

Map 5. *[John D. Barnhart and Dorothy L. Riker,* Indiana to 1816: The Colonial Period, *vol. 1,* The History of Indiana *(Indianapolis: Indiana Historical Bureau and the Indiana Historical Society, 1971).]*

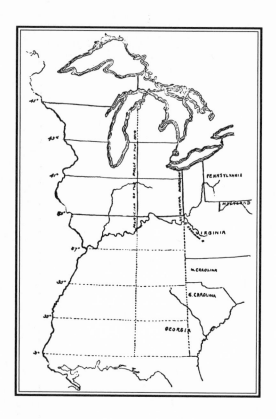

Map 6.   *Division of the West in the Ordinance of 1784. [Jay A. Barrett,* **Evolution of the Ordinance of 1787** *(New York: G.P. Putnam's Sons, 1891).]*

Map 7.   *The Northwest Territory as divided by the Northwest Ordinance (map by Bruce Baby).* [Peter S. Onuf, *"From Constitution to Higher Law: The Reinterpretation of the Northwest Ordinance,"* **Ohio History** 94 (1985), 6. *(Ohio Historical Society)]*

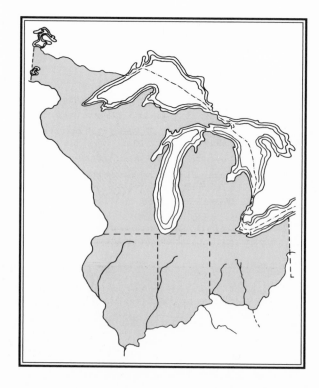

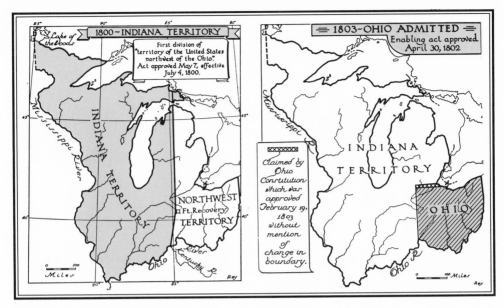

Map 8.   **Map 9.**

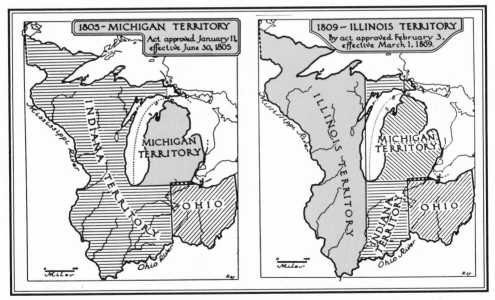

Map 10.   **Map 11.**

[Source for maps 8–16: R. Carlyle Buley, **The Old Northwest Pioneer Period,**
1815–1840 *(Indianapolis: Indiana Historical Society, 1950).]*

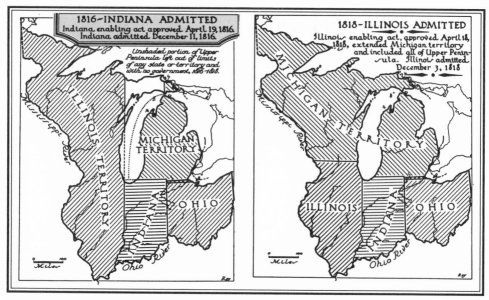

Map 12.

Map 13.

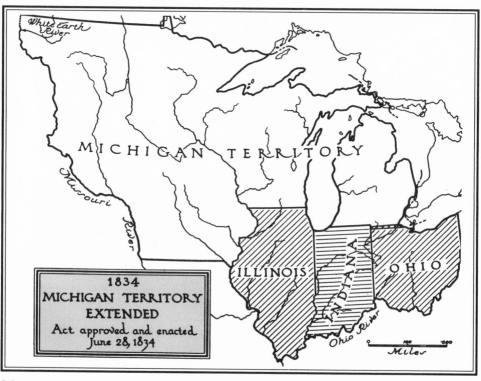

Map 14.

Map 15.

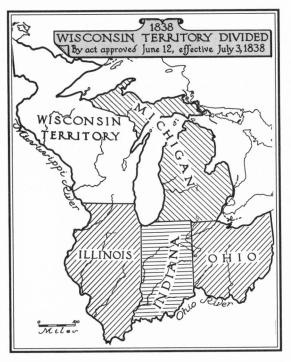

Map 16.

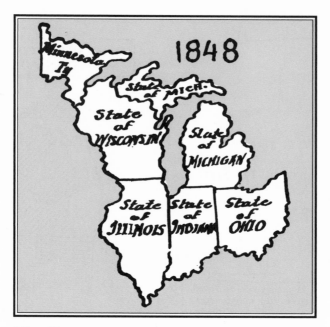

Map 17.

WISCONSIN ADMITTED

[Source for maps 17–18: **History of the Ordinance of 1787 and the Old Northwest Territory** *(Marietta, Ohio: Northwest Territory Celebration Commission, 1937).]*

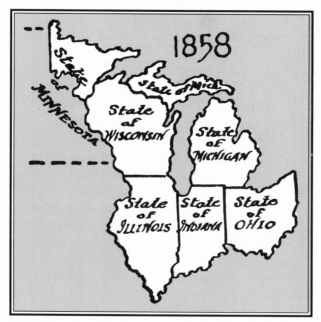

Map 18.

MINNESOTA ADMITTED

Putting the Ordinance to Work
in the Northwest

BY

PATRICK J. FURLONG

WHEN THE CONTINENTAL CONGRESS passed the Northwest Ordinance on July 13, 1787, it created only the outline of a territorial government. The fundamental principles of limited self-government and eventual statehood were clear enough, but how long the territorial period might last and how the largely unexplored expanse of territory would actually be governed could only be guessed. The creation of a government for the lands north and west of the Ohio River had long been neglected by the Congress, and it was spurred to action in 1787 more by the lobbying efforts of land speculators than by any concern for the well-being of the few thousand inhabitants scattered through the wilderness.

When the subject of government was mentioned in Congress, there was serious doubt that the westerners would be competent to govern themselves without firm direction from their betters in the long-settled states along the Atlantic seaboard. The only precedents available to the members of Congress were the royal instructions issued to colonial governors to advise and guide them in the exercise of their duties. The colonial assemblies had often objected to these instructions when they found themselves in opposition to the royal governors. Now that the colonies had formed a government of their own it might seem that the policies of the British Empire would be completely rejected, but there is no doubt that many of the delegates in Congress looked upon the western settlements very much as American colonies. True, under Thomas Jefferson's Ordinance of 1784 the principle was clearly established that the western territory would in time be admitted to the Union as states equal in every respect to the original thirteen states. This was reaffirmed in the Northwest Ordinance, but until there was a sufficient settled population in the West, Congress would rule supreme.[1]

The Northwest Ordinance was approved on July 13, 1787, but it was not until October 5 that the territorial officers were appointed. Meanwhile negotiations continued between members of Congress and the agents of the Ohio Company, who sought both favorable terms for land sales and influence in the selection of the territorial governor. The favored candidate was Samuel Holden Parsons, one of the leaders of the Ohio Company, but Congress was unwilling to accept him for the highest office in the new territory. He was named, however, as one of the three judges, despite the likelihood of a conflict between his judicial duties and his own extensive land interests. For reasons never clearly established, the company's chief lobbyist, Rev. Manasseh Cutler, then recommended the president of Congress, and so Arthur St. Clair became governor of the Northwest Territory. His appointment was for three years at a salary of $1,000 a year, with an additional $1,000 when he assumed the duties of superintendent of Indian affairs for the northern frontier.[2]

Arthur St. Clair was a Scottish officer who had remained in the colonies at the end of the French and Indian War and settled in western Pennsylvania. Although he held several county offices by appointment of the provincial government, St. Clair supported the patriot cause in 1775 and assumed command of a battalion of Pennsylvania troops. He rose to the rank of major general in the Continental Army, but his only independent command ended in defeat in 1777 when he abandoned Fort Ticonderoga to Gen. John Burgoyne's advancing army. St. Clair remained with the army until the end of the war and then settled in Philadelphia. He was always in need of a steady income, and he probably accepted the office of governor of the Northwest Territory because he needed the $2,000 a year. If this was his reason, he was often to regret his decision. Although other territorial officers were deeply engaged in land speculation, St. Clair was strictly honest and never involved himself in land dealings. He owned little more than the thousand-acre freehold needed to qualify as governor.[3]

The second ranking territorial official was the secretary, Winthrop Sargent, and he was closely involved in the affairs of the Ohio Company. Sargent, an elegant gentleman from Massachusetts, was a Harvard graduate, a former major in the Continental Army, and, more recently, a land surveyor in the West. No one ever denied his abilities, but many of his associates regarded him as arrogant and selfish. His salary as secretary was $750 a year, a sum which he soon found inadequate to cover the expenses of living and traveling in the West. In addition to General Parsons, the territorial judges were John Armstrong and James M. Varnum. Like St. Clair and Sargent, Varnum was also a former officer of the Continental Army, rising to brigadier general. At the time of his appointment he was a delegate in Congress from Rhode Island. Armstrong declined his judgeship, and in February 1788 the post was awarded to another land speculator, John Cleves Symmes, whose tangled land claims would trouble the Northwest Territory and its residents for years to come.[4]

Governor St. Clair was in no hurry to assume his new duties, and over the years his long absences from the territory were often the subject of criticism. He received his first formal instructions from Congress on October 26, directing him to attempt to make a treaty with the Indians to regulate trade and settle boundaries. Far more important were the contracts signed the following day between the board of treasury on behalf of Congress and Manasseh Cutler and Winthrop Sargent, who represented both the Ohio Company and another unidentified group of associates. The Ohio Company purchased 1,500,000 acres for one million dollars, while Cutler and Sargent purchased 750,000 acres for half a million dollars payable over a period of three years.[5]

Governor St. Clair journeyed as far west as Pittsburgh to investigate the chances of a conference with the Indians and then returned to Philadelphia. Secretary Sargent went off to New England to deal with the affairs of the Ohio Company. Meanwhile the government of the Northwest Territory existed only on paper, and the only symbol of lawful authority in all of the western country was Brig. Gen. Josiah Harmar and his small garrisons at Vincennes, the Falls of the Ohio, and Fort Harmar on the Ohio at the mouth of the Muskingum River. The new year brought still further delays and additional Indian troubles. The civil government of the territory seemed to matter only to the inhabitants, for the appointed officials lacked any sense of urgency. Governor St. Clair reached Fort Harmar on July 9, 1788, and established the territorial government on July 15 by a formal reading of the Northwest Ordinance and an address to the people of Marietta. An entire year passed between the adoption of the Ordinance by the Confederation Congress and the inauguration of the government in the West. It would be many months more before the territorial government extended to the most distant settlements at Kaskaskia and Cahokia on the banks of the Mississippi, nearly five hundred miles farther to the west.[6]

In his first speech as governor, St. Clair asserted that a well-administered government was the first of public blessings for any people. He noted that the new form of government he brought was only temporary, suited to the "state of infancy" of the western country. In language that might have been used by any colonial governor, St. Clair praised the "paternal attention" of Congress toward the inhabitants of the territory. The governor made the appropriate references to "reducing a country from a state of nature to a state of civilization" and to the "vast forest converted into arable fields, and cities rising in places . . . lately the habitations of wild beasts," and closed his address by admonishing the people to treat the Indians with Christian kindness. The inhabitants of Marietta replied with an even more flowery address in which they assured St. Clair that they were "fully satisfied with the system of our temporary government" and that they always treated the Indians "like friends, like brothers." It was indeed a happy occasion, but the cheerful speeches must not be taken too seriously. Both political disputes and bloody wars with the Indians would mark the growth of the Northwest Territory.[7]

Although the territorial government was now formally in effect, its power was only slowly extended across the vast expanse of wilderness within its jurisdiction. There were few maps and none of any detail or accuracy, and the governor's geographical information was often vague and contradictory. Most of the territory was controlled by potentially hostile Indians, while British troops continued to occupy Detroit and distant Michilimackinac to the north and British agents exercised great influence over the Shawnee, Miami, and other tribes living in the Wabash country and along the banks of the Miami River of the Lake (the modern Maumee River). Travel was slow, dangerous, and expensive, subject to all the perils of nature as well as occasional Indian attacks. There was mail service from Marietta to Pittsburgh, but elsewhere letters had to be carried by travelers or special messengers. By the summer of 1790 there was still no printing press anywhere in the territory, making it impossible to publish the laws except by having them read aloud in the courts. There were not enough manuscript copies for all of the magistrates. St. Clair was allocated money by Congress for negotiations with the Indians, but there was no appropriation for the civil government of the territory and no territorial taxes as yet. Fees and fines provided a small and unreliable revenue, and the territorial officials were often troubled by a lack of money to pay for their basic expenses. When the federal Constitution came into effect in 1789, Congress passed a law continuing the Northwest Ordinance in full effect, except to vest the power of appointment in the president and to direct the governor to report to him instead of to Congress as before.[8]

One of the most difficult problems facing the new territorial government concerned the French inhabitants of Vincennes, Cahokia, and Kaskaskia. Their support for George Rogers Clark during the War for Independence was not forgotten, and both Congress and St. Clair wished to safeguard their claims to lands which were supported by tradition and long occupation rather than by deeds or written sales contracts. Congress directed St. Clair in August of 1788 to visit Kaskaskia and settle the land claims there, but he did not reach that distant settlement until March of 1790. His winter journey from Marietta to Kaskaskia required more than ten weeks, with great delays from low water at the Falls of the Ohio and heavy ice which blocked the Mississippi. The governor found most of the residents ignorant and illiterate, but he also thought them "the gentlest, well-disposed people that can be imagined." Fortunately his French was adequate to talk with the residents and read their scant records, for as he told President Washington, he had to make translations of all of the laws and public documents himself because the territorial government had no money for translators. Isolated as he was in the wilderness, St. Clair lamented that he knew as little of the news of New York and Philadelphia as the man in the moon. "For pity sake," he asked Henry Knox, "send some newspapers, I never before thought them of any consequence—they will now be a great treat."[9]

There was also the essential routine business of the territory. For the American inhabitants the most immediate symbol of government was the creation of a new county. The process began with Washington County on July 26, 1788. It stretched from the Ohio River northward to Lake Erie, and from the Pennsylvania line westward to the

Cuyahoga River in the north and the Scioto River in the south, with Marietta as the county seat of government. A new county meant the appointment of judges, justices of the peace, sheriffs, coroners, clerks, and recorders of deeds, as well as officers for the militia. On January 4, 1790, the governor established Hamilton County, changed the name of the village of Losantiville to the more imposing and elegant Cincinnati, and made it the county seat. While at Kaskaskia, St. Clair created an additional county and named it for himself, and at Vincennes Winthrop Sargent established Knox County and appointed its officers. Few citizens had frequent cause to deal with territorial government, but from time to time anyone might find himself before some officer of the county, whether as plaintiff or defendant, witness or heir, militia private or property owner filing a deed.[10]

The governor and the three judges constituted the legislature under the first stage of territorial government, but there was a troublesome ambiguity in the Ordinance itself. Did their power to "adopt and publish" laws from the original thirteen states mean that they could only select particular state laws in their entirety, or could they devise distinct laws more appropriate for the circumstances of the western territory? The governor and the judges disagreed for years on this fundamental question of the territorial constitution. St. Clair argued that they were limited to selecting from the laws of the states, while Parsons and Varnum, and later Symmes, held that they could write new laws if no appropriate existing law could be found among the state statutes. The governor reluctantly complied with the majority opinion, so that the territory would not be without the essential protection of written law, but the issue remained in dispute.

The territorial judges were all lawyers, and the governor was not. However, after five years of argument Congress disallowed the laws, and St. Clair and the judges were compelled to adopt a legal code for the Northwest Territory by selecting the most suitable laws from the statute books of the thirteen original states. This new code of laws was adopted at a public legislative session held at Cincinnati from May 29 until August 15, 1795. The laws, thirty-five in number, were ordered printed for the use of judges and justices of the peace throughout the territory, and from this time there was no little argument about the legal forms of territorial law making.[11]

Enforcement of the laws of the United States within the territory caused occasional difficulty. There was no federal court for the Northwest Territory, and Governor St. Clair argued that federal laws under the new Constitution should not be applied within the territory unless Congress explicitly provided that they should extend beyond the states. The constitutional question was of considerable interest, but the immediate problem was the collection of taxes on distilled spirits, whether whiskey or brandy. The resistance of many of the farmers of western Pennsylvania led to the Whiskey Rebellion of 1794, and St. Clair wished to avoid both disorder and the bad example which would result from insisting on the validity of a law which he realized he could not enforce. There was no governmental power within the territory capable of collecting the whiskey tax, whatever the governor and the judges believed the law to be. Attorney General William Bradford and Secretary of the Treasury Oliver Wolcott were emphatic in their opinion that the whiskey tax and all other federal laws did indeed apply to the residents of the Northwest Territory, but while their legal opinion swayed the governor, it did not establish an effective system to collect federal taxes in the wilderness.[12]

Congress reserved the sale of western lands for itself, and the territorial government had no voice in the matter. Problems resulting from land sales, however, often perplexed Governor St. Clair and the judges. Indian troubles and administrative bungling delayed some surveys for years, and regular government land sales to individual purchasers did not begin until October 1796. The enormous purchases by the Ohio Company, by Cutler and

Sargent, and by Symmes all led to prolonged disputes. The great speculators made promises which they were unable or unwilling to keep, and the aggrieved settlers appealed to the territorial government for redress. St. Clair personally received many letters from French officers he had known during the War for Independence who purchased lands from the Scioto Company. They settled on the banks of the Ohio in a town named Gallipolis. However, promises made in Paris went unfulfilled in the wilderness, and they were a miserably unhappy group. Their land titles were the subject of dispute and litigation for years, and Winthrop Sargent, the territorial secretary, was one of the leading land speculators involved in the transaction. Congress settled much of the difficulty with legislative land grants in 1795, but additional claims continued for several years more.[13]

The million acres of land between the Great Miami and Little Miami rivers purchased by John Cleves Symmes caused even greater disputes. Symmes was not able to pay for the lands as called for by his contract and either carelessly or fraudulently sold land he did not own or had already sold to others. To confuse the business even further, he sat as a judge in suits concerning his own land speculations, and he became one of the most hated men in the Northwest Territory. St. Clair and Sargent both became exasperated with Symmes and argued with him about the legal business of the territory as well as his real estate dealings. The land dispute about the Symmes Purchase lasted throughout the territorial period and resulted in the financial ruin of Symmes.[14]

From the very beginning the Northwest Territory was troubled by hostilities with the Indians all along the Ohio. The basic reason for the conflict was obvious enough—the ever increasing pressure of white settlers on Indian lands. Despite the high hopes of Congress and later the Washington administration, there was never any realistic possibility of a peaceful solution. Neither Indians nor white Americans would give up their determination to possess the rich

lands of the Northwest, and men on both sides were prepared to kill for their beliefs. In legal terms the government
of the Northwest Territory had very little to do with Indian
relations, but in October 1787 Congress joined the office of
Superintendent of Indian Affairs for the Northern Department to the office of Governor of the Northwest Territory, giving St. Clair full responsibility for negotiations
with all of the Indian tribes. From the beginning he devoted greater attention to Indian matters than to the civil
affairs of the territory, and he believed that he had achieved
a significant agreement with the Fort Harmar treaties of
January 1789. The respite was brief, and conflicts were
numerous and bloody all the way from the Muskingum
valley to Kaskaskia on the Mississippi.[15]

The stories of General Harmar's unsuccessful expedi-
tion to the upper Wabash country in 1790 and of General St.
Clair's disastrous defeat in the same region in 1791 are well
known. St. Clair led the better part of the United States
Army into battle, not in his capacity as governor of the
territory but under a separate commission, issued in March
of 1791, as major general of the regular army. Winthrop
Sargent also returned to active service as colonel and adju-
tant general, and throughout 1791 the two chief officers of
the territory were fully engaged in their military duties.
Sargent's "Journal of Executive Proceedings" for the year
shows only a few civil appointments, one dispute with the
judges on a matter of law, and one lengthy exchange of
correspondence with Symmes about his land grant. St.
Clair spent the period from January to May of 1792 in
Philadelphia defending his conduct as general, and civil
administration passed to Sargent as acting governor during his absence.[16]

St. Clair was replaced as army commander in the
spring of 1792 by Gen. Anthony Wayne, who operated
independently of the territorial government. St. Clair and
Sargent attended to their civil duties while Wayne drilled a
new army and led it to a complete victory in 1794 at Fallen
Timbers, on the outskirts of the modern Toledo, Ohio. At

Greenville the following year Wayne compelled the leaders of all of the northwestern tribes to agree to a treaty which opened a vast tract of land for white settlement, including more than half of the modern state of Ohio and a small portion of southeastern Indiana. Peace meant that land surveyors could return to their task and that settlers could journey westward concerned about making a living rather than keeping their scalps.

Where there had once been only a few scattered settlements, all more worried about Indian attacks than politics, there were soon thousands of secure settlers who regarded the appointed rulers under the first stage of territorial government as no longer suited for their improved condition. Governor St. Clair, however, argued still that the westerners were unready for representative government. This fundamental disagreement set the tone of political dispute for the remainder of the territorial period. St. Clair held to the idea that the people would benefit from the firm exercise of authority, while a growing number of ambitious politicians demanded first an elected assembly and then statehood as soon as possible.[17]

The population of the Northwest Territory increased rapidly, from an estimated 3,200 in 1793 to 10,328 in Hamilton County alone by 1798. The Ordinance provided that an elected assembly should be established when the population of adult free men reached 5,000. The settlement of Chillicothe in 1796 marked the beginning of rapid growth in the mid-Scioto valley, as pioneers now felt safe to move northward from the Ohio River. Nathaniel Massie and Thomas Worthington emerged as the political leaders of the Chillicothe residents, and they were often in disagreement with Governor St. Clair. The settlers of Connecticut's Western Reserve on the shores of Lake Erie, led by Moses Cleaveland, virtually ignored the territorial government and played no role in its politics.[18]

Governor St. Clair appears to have been personally popular during the early years of his administration, respected for his honesty and his agreeable manners. Although a believer in firm and paternal government, he was not regarded as arrogant or overbearing, and his dreadful defeat at the hands of the Indians was not generally held against him. In the peaceful years after the Treaty of Greenville, however, antagonisms appeared and multiplied. The governor believed that there was no lawyer in the territory willing to serve as attorney general, but when he appointed his son to the position in 1796 there was naturally talk of favoritism. Arthur St. Clair, Jr., seems to have performed his duties competently and without injury to the treasury, but territorial politics was becoming a very serious business indeed. The people, or at least those who claimed to speak for the people, wanted to elect a representative assembly, and the governor believed in his heart that they were not yet ready to govern themselves, even in the limited fashion prescribed for the second stage of territorial government under the Ordinance.[19]

Governor St. Clair was an old man by frontier standards, sixty years old in 1796, and he often suffered from the gout as well as occasional other sickness. His family and his business interests remained in Ligonier, about forty miles east of Pittsburgh, and his long absences had often troubled Winthrop Sargent, who became acting governor whenever St. Clair was not within the boundaries of the territory. At times Sargent did not learn for some weeks where St. Clair might be or which of them should exercise the powers of the governor. The problem was particularly acute in June of 1796, when Sargent hurried to Detroit to establish the civil government there as soon as the British handed over the fort to American authority. Governor St. Clair remained ill at his Pennsylvania home for many months, and Sargent served both as secretary and acting governor for much of the period from May 1796 until he departed to become governor of the new Mississippi Territory in May 1798. For part of this period, however, the territory had two men acting as governor, St. Clair at Cincinnati and Sargent at Detroit, each ignorant of the other's actions. As he completed his duties as secretary of the

Northwest Territory, Winthrop Sargent compiled a memorandum showing that Governor St. Clair had been absent
from the territory for more than five and a half years of his
eleven years as governor. Sargent calculated that his service
as acting governor should have brought him additional
salary of $6,939.03, which of course he never received.[20]

The Northwest Territory did not have a fixed seat of
government until 1798. The capital was wherever Governor
St. Clair or Acting Governor Sargent happened to be, with
Marietta assumed to be their customary "home." When he
was well enough to return to his duties in 1798, St. Clair at
last brought his family west with him and settled at Cincinnati, which thereby became the seat of government. After
more than three years of peace and rapid immigration, the
population of the territory was clearly more than the 5,000
adult free males required for the second stage of territorial
government, and St. Clair accordingly issued a call for
elections in October. The voting, by open outcry, took place
in December at one town in each of the territory's nine
counties. Hamilton County was allotted five members,
Washington County two, and the others one each. The
fourteen representatives assembled at Cincinnati in February 1799 "to do and perform what is required of them for
the benefit of the People and the good government" of the
Northwest Territory.[21]

The representative stage of territorial government
commenced with cheerful oratory from Governor St. Clair.
The representatives were able only to organize themselves
and to nominate ten candidates for the legislative council.
Substantive business had to await the selection of the five
councilors by President Adams, and the real work of the
assembly did not begin until it reconvened at Cincinnati in
September. In his address the governor recalled his long
dispute with the judges about adopting or making laws for
the territory, laws which he now described as of "very
doubtful obligation." Under the Ordinance the authority of
the general assembly to devise and pass laws shaped to the
particular needs of the western territory was beyond ques-

tion, as was the governor's absolute veto. He suggested the repeal of all of the existing territorial laws and their replacement with a new legal code of unquestioned constitutionality. St. Clair closed his address by saying how pleasant it was that "the people are now about to legislate for themselves." His desire for political harmony was doomed to early and frequent disappointment.[22]

Both houses of the assembly met on September 25, 1799, and the governor opened the session with another formal address. He again urged the adoption of an entirely new code of laws and added a plea for enactment of a territorial tax. Remarkable as it may seem, the Northwest Territory had existed for twelve years without the collection of any territorial tax upon its residents. The governor, secretary, and judges had received their salaries from the general government and complained often about the lack of money for their expenses. Now at last it was possible to remedy such problems by action of the general assembly. In its reply the council voiced its gratitude for the system of territorial government so "full of wisdom and benignity" as well as the "virtue, integrity and talents" of Governor St. Clair. The house of representatives echoed with its own fulsome praise and "unbounded confidence" in the governor. Both houses promised to promote morality, suppress vice, encourage religion and education, and improve the militia. Not one word suggested any hint of political animosity, but strong differences of opinion soon appeared with the election of the territory's first delegate to Congress. William Henry Harrison, a young Virginian of an eminent political family and a former aide to Gen. Anthony Wayne, had been appointed secretary in succession to Winthrop Sargent, and now the assembly chose him as delegate by a margin of one vote over Arthur St. Clair, Jr. The majority was willing to praise the governor in a formal address, but not to elect his son to any higher office.[23]

The general assembly remained in session at Cincinnati for two months and passed thirty-nine laws on topics ranging from the taxation of land to the encouragement of killing wolves. Most of the business was tedious rather than controversial, and the assembly worked in the usual pattern of American legislatures by appointing a large number of select and standing committees. Edward Tiffin, who was chosen as speaker of the house, and Massie and Worthington were the most active of the elected members, while Jacob Burnet played a leading role in the council in drafting laws. The assembly endeavored to create new counties and relocate county seats, but the governor firmly insisted that he held exclusive power to establish counties and vetoed six bills in which the assembly attempted to seize the initiative. The assembly replied with a petition to Congress against the exercise of a total veto by the governor, and the controversy troubled the remaining years of St. Clair's service as governor. There was a distinctly partisan dispute when the majority approved a highly Federalist address in praise of President Adams written by Jacob Burnet. Five firmly Republican members of the house voted against the address, and while they were in the minority in 1799, their numbers and influence increased in the next assembly. Massie and Worthington, both Virginians and both residents of the Chillicothe region, became the leading members of the opposition to Governor St. Clair and leading advocates of early statehood for the eastern portion of the territory.[24]

Division of the Northwest Territory was provided by the Ordinance itself, but the timing and manner became matters of great argument. Governor St. Clair wanted to split the territory into three portions, with seats of government at Marietta, Cincinnati, and Vincennes. This division would have the advantage of separating the well-populated districts around Chillicothe and Cincinnati and thereby keeping both the eastern and middle portions in the territorial condition for many years. The Chillicothe Republicans wanted to divide the territory into two portions, drawing the line to the west of Cincinnati, assuring that the eastern region would soon attain the 60,000 residents needed to become a state. Harrison as a territorial delegate could speak in the House of Representatives but not vote, but even without a vote he managed to influence the deliberations of Congress. In 1800 a Federalist majority decided to split the territory into two portions, creating the Indiana Territory in the west, while the smaller but far more populous eastern district remained as the Northwest Territory. St. Clair and his friends were defeated, and Harrison was able to assist St. Clair's opponents even further by moving the territorial capital to their home ground at Chillicothe. The political disputes there became very intense indeed, while William Henry Harrison was appointed governor of the new Indiana Territory and moved to Vincennes to establish his government in peace and harmony.[25]

The final years of the Northwest Territory were marked by bitter political arguments which quickly became highly personal. Governor St. Clair was a Federalist and a devoted adherent to the principle of firm government for the welfare of the people, whether they wanted such government or not. Nathaniel Massie and Thomas Worthington were much younger, ambitious for landed wealth and political power, firmly Republican in their politics. In their view Arthur St. Clair was an old tyrant who should be overthrown for the good of the people. There were also intense regional differences between the Virginia Republicans around Chillicothe and the older and more varied populations near Cincinnati and Marietta. Governor St. Clair was not without friends, particularly at Cincinnati, but he had never been much of a politician, and he was not about to change his ways at the age of sixty-four.[26]

The elections for representatives in the general assembly, held in October of 1800, were heatedly contested on a partisan basis. There were no organized political parties in the territory, but supporters and opponents of the governor were known to the voters through the newspapers as well as through impromptu oratory. The election results were not entirely satisfactory for either side, and the general assembly convened at Chillicothe in November with the balance of power still unsettled. Most of the governor's long opening speech concerned such safe topics as divine blessings on the territory and a more Christian attitude toward the Indians. St. Clair offended many, however, with his remarks about the disputed question of county seats and more perhaps when he spoke of bribery and corruption tainting the recent elections. He recommended written ballots in place of viva voce voting, which required each voter to announce his choice so that all could hear him. Even so, he would probably have emerged unscathed had he not closed by noting the "vilist calumnies, and the grossest falsehoods" which were being circulated among the people by unnamed evildoers who presumably sat among the audience.[27]

Governor St. Clair's address brought all of the personal and political issues growing out of his own views and policies into an arena where he would become the sacrificial victim. Both chambers of the assembly sent formal replies which deplored accusations against the governor, but the answer from the house left little doubt that some representatives believed the governor guilty as anonymously charged. The words were kind enough, "manifest purity of your intentions . . . unprovoked attacks of the wicked and malevolent," but not entirely convincing, particularly as they were included by a vote of twelve for and six against. Because his appointment as governor had not yet been renewed by President Adams, St. Clair prorogued the assembly in order to prevent the Republican-inclined secretary, Charles William Byrd, from becoming acting governor. St. Clair's action, very much in the tradition of those of colonial governors in the face of a hostile assembly, roused the Republicans to greater efforts, and in the last days of the session they pushed a resolution in favor of statehood through the house by a vote of nine to eight and ordered five hundred copies printed for circulation throughout the territory. St. Clair's enemies also tried and failed to persuade the president to deny St. Clair another term as governor, but he was greatly embarrassed by his belated reappointment and by the further delay before its approval by the Senate.[28]

The Republicans of the Northwest Territory were greatly heartened by the victory of Thomas Jefferson in 1800, but they were dismayed when the census showed a population of 45,365, only three-quarters of the number required to form a state under the provisions of the Ordinance. Governor St. Clair opened the 1801 session of the general assembly with a rather conciliatory address, speaking of such safe topics as settling land titles within the Symmes Purchase and improving the militia. The council replied with congratulations on his reappointment as governor, while the house, although polite, said nothing about his new term. St. Clair asked for increased taxes, and the assembly declined. A number of routine measures passed without difficulty, but efforts to move the territorial capital away from Chillicothe and to divide the territory anew brought fierce dispute and a demonstration in the streets of the capital which the governor termed a riot. Massie, Worthington, and Tiffin were the Republican leaders, and they were more determined than ever to advance the territory to statehood as soon as possible and then to win control of the new government. Massie and Tiffin argued, constitutionally, that any further division of the territory would violate the Northwest Ordinance and, politically, that the effort was an obvious scheme to delay statehood.[29]

The law seeking a division of the territory was narrowly adopted, and St. Clair forwarded it to Congress with an unconvincing explanation that the measure was not intended to delay statehood. Both parties sent petitions to Congress, and Thomas Worthington journeyed to Washington to argue the Republican cause in person. Further division of the territory was overwhelmingly rejected, and Worthington stayed on to argue for early statehood, describing the territorial government as something better suited for a Spanish colony. The Republican Congress, not at all sympathetic to Governor St. Clair, decided in April

1802 to permit a constitutional convention for the state of Ohio, despite the admittedly inadequate population of the territory. Politics prevailed over the requirements of the Northwest Ordinance, and to emphasize the victory of the Chillicothe Republicans the territorial assembly was excluded from any role in forming the state government. The members of the lower house had been elected, as the Ordinance required, by adult male property owners, and the Republicans asserted that they were not truly representative of the people of the territory because non-landowners had been excluded. In reality the Republicans were not confident of their ability to control the general assembly, and so they arranged to work around it. St. Clair and his friends were utterly defeated.[30]

Worthington, Massie, and friends moved forward eagerly with the political efforts necessary to win control of the constitutional convention and assure statehood for Ohio and offices for themselves. Although St. Clair was now a lame duck politically if not legally, they were unwilling to allow him to finish his term as territorial governor in peace. Massie wrote to Secretary of State James Madison and Worthington, to President Jefferson accusing the governor of using his veto to deny the will of the people, of extorting fees for licenses, and of favoring his son with appointment to office. St. Clair also wrote to the president, defending his conduct and denying all of the charges against him. He knew well enough that his days as governor were few, but he hoped to retire in dignity. "I have given up the best years of my life, at the expense of my health and fortune," he wrote, explaining that he sought only to advance the welfare of the people of the territory. He had tried, he told Jefferson, to guide the West while it was in "a colonial state" and to teach its residents the habits of industry, virtue, and obedience to the laws. His financial losses while governor he could endure, St. Clair lamented, "but a removal can not take place without deeply affecting my reputation."

Governor St. Clair received no answer from President

Jefferson. The charges made against him were trivial enough, but his own outspoken political principles provided even better evidence for his enemies. When the convention to prepare the Ohio constitution met at Chillicothe in November 1802, the governor asked to speak to the delegates. He spoke in paternal fashion as one who had guided the Northwest Territory through many years of danger and expansion. He noted the popular habit of complaining of oppression even where it did not exist and asserted that he had governed "with gentleness, and with one single view, the good of the whole" while the Northwest was in "the colonial state." Then, just as so many other Federalists before him, St. Clair lamented the "party rage" which threatened the entire nation, by which he meant the Republicans, for Federalists thought of themselves as "the friends of order" rather than a political party. He went on to criticize the enabling law passed by the Republican Congress in the most severe terms, calling it degrading and "a nullity" which should be rejected as unconstitutional.[31]

Reports of the governor's remarks were quickly sent to Washington, and before the end of November the administration decided to remove St. Clair from office. James Madison wrote the letter, describing Jefferson's judgment that St. Clair's "intemperance and indecorum of language" toward the Congress was an offense "grossly violating" the rules of proper conduct for a territorial governor. As a result, "your Commission of Governor of the North Western Territory shall cease on the receipt of this notification." Charles William Byrd, as territorial secretary, became acting governor for the remaining weeks of the territory's existence, although he had for some months refused to perform his secretarial duties. St. Clair sent Madison a bitter letter thanking the president for "discharging me from an office I was heartily tired of, about six weeks sooner than I had" expected. In his last action as governor, Arthur St. Clair defended his remarks to the convention, condemned Congress for abusing the rights of the citizens of the Northwest, and assured Madison that his letter had been received with derision. So ended the Northwest Territory, as Gov. Edward Tiffin inaugurated the government of Ohio at Chillicothe on March 1, 1803.[32]

The Ohio constitution showed several signs of the political struggles within the Northwest Territory. Surprisingly, there was considerable support for allowing blacks to vote, but in the end the delegates decided that any white man who paid taxes would be allowed to vote. Property requirements for holding office were also eliminated. Both slavery and indentured servitude were strictly forbidden. The Virginia Republicans who controlled the convention had all struggled against an appointed governor and his appointed officials, so the Ohio constitution provided that a vetoless governor with little patronage would be popularly elected for a two-year term and that the judges and all county and township officials would also be elected. The legislature, with the lower house elected annually and the upper for only two years, would be powerful but firmly under popular control. The encouragement of religion and education introduced by the Northwest Ordinance were continued. Despite their devotion to democratic ideals, however, the political realism of the Republican forces impelled them to put the constitution into effect without submitting it to the people for their approval. They were still afraid that St. Clair and his friends might make a last desperate effort to postpone statehood, and they took no chances.[33]

Gov. William Henry Harrison established the government of the Indiana Territory in 1800 amid general rejoicing. Harrison was young, energetic, and affable, and he had learned well from watching St. Clair's mistakes. Unlike his notorious father-in-law, Judge Symmes, Harrison avoided land speculation and was always regarded as honest. He was highly successful for nine years in making treaties with the Indians to open additional lands for settlement. When Indian resistance reappeared under Tenskwatawa (called the Prophet by the Americans) and his brother Tecumseh, General Harrison led his troops to a bloody victory at Tippecanoe in 1811. St. Clair had often been away from his territorial duties, but Harrison moved with his family to Vincennes and built an elegant brick mansion which symbolized his attachment to Indiana as well as his considerable wealth.

The representative stage of territorial government came early and easily to the Indiana Territory in 1804, for Harrison was too shrewd a politician to oppose a measure so well liked by so many people. The most troublesome issue was a prolonged effort to alter or to evade Article Six of the Northwest Ordinance and introduce black slavery to the territory. Many of the better sort of settlers from Virginia and Kentucky wanted to use slave labor to bring their heavily forested lands into agricultural use, and poorer settlers, especially those of mid-Atlantic or New England origin, firmly opposed slavery because it gave an unfair advantage to those with the money to buy Negroes. The first elected legislature voted in 1805 to allow anyone who purchased a slave outside Indiana to bring the slave into the territory and bind him by indenture for an unlimited period. Slaves who refused to accept the terms of the indenture could be removed from the territory and sold. Young slaves and children of slaves were bound for labor until they reached specified ages ranging from twenty-eight to thirty-five. Indentures as long as ninety-nine years were recorded, and Governor Harrison was among the prominent residents who held black "servants" who were really slaves. In 1807 the legislature formally asked Congress to repeal Article Six and make slavery legal in the territory, but the request was never brought to a vote in Washington. The census of 1810 recorded 237 "slaves" in Indiana, despite Article Six.

Antislavery sentiment was increasing, particularly in the southeastern part of the territory, and from late 1807 onward it provided an issue for the growing opposition to the governor. By 1808 Harrison's opponents, led by Jonathan Jennings, had control of the assembly. The governor remained personally popular and avoided the public disputes which had undermined St. Clair's position. The growing Indian troubles distracted both the governor and his rivals from ordinary politics, and when the United States declared war in June of 1812 Gen. William Henry Harrison led the forces which defended the northwestern frontier from the British and their Indian allies. Harrison was forced to resign as governor, and when peace was restored in 1815 it was obvious that the Indiana Territory would soon become a state. Jennings and his friends dominated the statehood movement and faced no organized opposition. The Indiana constitution of 1816 included a strong antislavery clause and gave the vote to all white male citizens over twenty-one. The governor was popularly elected for a three-year term, and the office was significantly stronger than in Ohio. There were no property requirements for any office. Free education at all levels through the state university was proclaimed but not financed. In its sixteen years as a territory Indiana had been largely free of the bitter legal and political arguments which had characterized Ohio. Much of the credit belongs to Governor Harrison, a politician wise enough to give way gracefully but not too quickly as the opposition forces gained votes. But there is something beyond individual personality and political circumstance. The routines of territorial government were becoming familiar to people and public officials alike, and the legal framework was clearly established. There was no longer any significant question about the meaning of the various provisions of the Northwest Ordinance, although arguments over slavery were not entirely settled.[34]

The Illinois Territory was separated from Indiana in 1809, and it was soon caught up in Indian conflict and then the war with Britain. The only territorial governor, Ninian Edwards, was a Kentuckian appointed because he was not involved with any of the political factions in Illinois. Like Harrison he was regarded as rather aristocratic in manner, but also like Harrison he had the ability to deal with a wide variety of people on friendly terms. Edwards also imitated Harrison in the ease with which he acceded to demands for territorial elections in 1812, although the population was far below the required level. After the war there was a swelling demand for statehood, although the only principled issue was the widespread objection to the governor's absolute veto over legislative actions as provided by the Northwest Ordinance. As one furious editorial noted, the territorial regime was "a species of despotism" while another remarked that "to remain longer in this negative situation . . . is too humiliating for a people who possess the talents and means of self government."

Governor Edwards had no desire to stand against the expressed will of the people and joined the effort for early statehood despite the legal requirements. Daniel Pope Cook, an ambitious lawyer and newspaper editor, and his uncle Nathaniel Pope, who was the territory's delegate in Congress, led the campaign. Pope's great achievement was to alter the boundary set by the Northwest Ordinance and move the state line some forty miles northward, thus insuring that the Chicago portage and any economic development on the banks of the Chicago River would be in Illinois rather than Wisconsin. Pope also managed to reduce the population requirement from 60,000 to 40,000, and Edwards simply faked the census returns when it appeared that there were only 34,620 people in the Illinois Territory. Indentured servitude had been permitted under the territorial government, and the constitutional convention of 1818 heatedly debated the slavery question. The final document forbade the introduction of slaves or indentured servants into the state but upheld existing contracts and permitted slavery until 1825, only if the slaves were employed at saltworks. In other respects the Illinois constitution followed the now familiar pattern for statehood under the Northwest Ordinance.[35]

The Michigan Territory lasted longer than the other territorial governments under the Northwest Ordinance, from 1805 until 1837, but for much of this period there was only a scant American population. The few thousand residents near Detroit stirred extensive political quarrels involving Gov. William Hull and the judges in 1807, but the war which brought the British capture of Detroit pushed politics aside until 1815. By then, however, two persistent and troublesome issues were already agitated, the first bank charter in the West and the dispute over the location of the boundary between Michigan and Ohio. Hull was ruined by his cowardly surrender of Detroit, and Gen. Lewis Cass replaced him as governor in 1813. Cass was far more able as a soldier and a politician and remained governor until he was appointed secretary of war in 1831. Governor Cass put the question of an elected assembly and the second stage of territorial government to a vote in 1818, but the impoverished residents decided against it because of the expense. Despite this rejection, Congress authorized the election of a territorial delegate in 1819. Four years later Congress made a special provision for local elections to nominate members of a legislative council, a system which continued until statehood although it had originally been considered only temporary. Michigan never officially entered the representative stage of territorial government as provided by the Northwest Ordinance, although it had a functioning substitute. Railroads, banks, the Ohio boundary, and statehood were the leading political issues in Michigan by the mid-1830s, and the legal framework contained in the Ordinance of 1787 was rarely mentioned. Ohio and Michigan surveyors exchanged shots in 1835, and later that year a Michigan deputy sheriff was stabbed while trying to arrest an Ohio man in Toledo. Congress finally settled the dispute, clearing the way for Michigan to become a state in 1837, although the constitution was written and a legislature had been elected and had convened almost two years earlier.[36]

The Wisconsin Territory was the last to be formed within the original boundaries of the Northwest Territory, established in 1836 as Michigan made its tangled way to statehood. There was an elected assembly from the beginning in Wisconsin, and by the time of its creation there were no longer any legal or political arguments about the meaning of the Northwest Ordinance, which had been passed by the Confederation Congress half a century earlier.[37] The patterns of territorial government were well settled, the necessary legal precedents were firmly established, and personal and local political issues dominated the attention of voters and legislators alike. The Northwest Ordinance had become a matter of historical interest rather than political debate.

APPENDIX

The Ordinance of 1784
By the UNITED STATES in
CONGRESS assembled, April 23, 1784

CONGRESS resumed the consideration of the report of a committee on a plan for a temporary government of the western territory, which being amended, was agreed to as follows:

Resolved, That so much of the territory ceded or to be ceded by individual states to the United States, as is already purchased or shall be purchased of the Indian inhabitants, and offered for sale by Congress, shall be divided into distinct states in the following manner, as nearly as such cessions will admit; that is to say, by parallels of latitude, so that each state shall comprehend from north to south two degrees of latitude, beginning to count from the completion of forty five degrees north of the equator; and by meridians of longitude, one of which shall pass through the lowest point of the rapids of Ohio, and the other through the western cape of the mouth of the great Kanhaway; but the territory eastward of this last meridian, between the Ohio, Lake Erie, and Pennsylvania, shall be one state, whatsoever may be its comprehension of latitude. That which may lie beyond the completion of the 45th degree between the said meridians shall make part of the state adjoining it on the south; and that part of the Ohio, which is between the same meridians coinciding nearly with the parallel of 39° shall be substituted so far in lieu of that parallel as a boundary line.

That the settlers on any territory so purchased and offered for sale shall, either on their own petition or on the order of Congress, receive authority from them, with appointments of time and place, for their free males of full age within the limits of their state to meet together, for the purpose of establishing a temporary government, to adopt the constitution and laws of any one of the original states; so that such laws nevertheless shall be subject to alteration by their ordinary legislature; and to erect, subject to a like alteration, counties, townships, or other divisions, for the election of members for their legislature.

That when any such state shall have acquired twenty thousand free inhabitants, on giving due proof thereof to Congress, they shall receive from them authority with appointments of time and place, to call a Convention of representatives to establish a permanent constitution and government for themselves. Provided that both the temporary and permanent governments be established on these principles as their basis.

First. That they shall for ever remain a part of this confederacy of the United States of America

Second. That they shall be subject to the articles of confederation in all those cases in which the original states shall be so subject, and to all the acts and ordinances of the United States in Congress assembled, conformable thereto.

Third. That they in no case shall interfere with the primary disposal of the soil by the United States in Congress assembled, nor with the ordinances and regulations which Congress may find necessary for securing the title in such soil to the bona fide purchasers.

Fourth. That they shall be subject to pay a part of the federal debts contracted or to be contracted, to be apportioned on them by Congress, according to the same common rule and measure by which apportionments thereof shall be made on the other states.

Fifth. That no tax shall be imposed on lands the property of the United States.

Sixth. That their respective governments shall be republican.

Seventh. That the lands of non resident proprietors shall in no case be taxed higher than those of residents within any new state, before the admission thereof to a vote by its delegates in Congress.

That whensoever any of the said states shall have of free inhabitants, as many as shall then be in any one the least numerous of the thirteen original states, such state shall be admitted by its delegates into the Congress of the United States, on an equal footing with the said original states; provided the consent of so many states in Congress is first obtained as may at the time be competent to such admission. And in order to adapt [*sic*] the said articles of confederation to the state of Congress when its numbers shall be thus increased, it shall be proposed to the legislatures of the states, originally parties thereto, to require the assent of two thirds of the United States in Congress assembled, in all those cases wherein by the said articles, the assent of nine states is now required, which being agreed to by them shall be binding on the new states. Until such admission by their Delegates into Congress, any of the said states after the establishment of their temporary government shall have authority to keep a member in Congress, with a right of debating, but not of voting.

That measures not inconsistent with the principles of the confederation, and necessary for the preservation of peace and good order among the settlers in any of the said new states, until they shall assume a temporary government as aforesaid, may from time to time be taken by the United States in Congress assembled.

That the preceding articles shall be formed into a charter of compact; shall be duly executed by the President of the United States in Congress assembled, under his hand, and the seal of the United States; shall be promulgated; and shall stand as fundamental constitutions between the thirteen original states, and each of the several states now newly described, unalterable from and after the sale of any part of the territory of such state, pursuant to this resolve, but by the joint consent of the United States in Congress assembled, and of the particular state within which such alteration is proposed to be made.

CHARLES THOMSON, Secretary

Text from *Virginia Gazette*, under the dateline "Annapolis May 6." This text was obviously printed from the two-leaf publication of the Ordinance of 1784 issued by authority of Congress, bearing the same title, and being circulated by Thomson. It varies from that in the manuscript Journals of Congress only in spelling and punctuation and, of course, in the fact that the latter lacks title, preamble, and attest.[1]

Notes

The Northwest Ordinance from the Perspective of the Frontier

1. See Gordon S. Wood, ed., *The Rising Glory of America, 1760–1820* (New York: G. Braziller, 1971), introduction; Ralph Lerner, "Commerce and Character: The Anglo-American as New-Model Man," *William and Mary Quarterly*, 3d ser., 36 (1979): 3–26; Drew R. McCoy, *The Elusive Republic: Political Economy in Jeffersonian America* (Chapel Hill: University of North Carolina Press for the Institute of Early American History and Culture, 1980); Peter S. Onuf, "Liberty, Development, and Union: Visions of the West in the 1780s," *William and Mary Quarterly*, 3d ser., 43 (1986): 179–213; Thomas Slaughter, *The Whiskey Rebellion: Frontier Epilogue to the American Revolution* (New York: Oxford University Press, 1986); Andrew R. L. Cayton, *The Frontier Republic: Ideology and Politics in the Ohio Country, 1780–1825* (Kent, Ohio: Kent State University Press, 1986), chapter 2.

2. Robert F. Berkhofer, Jr., "Jefferson, the Ordinance of 1784, and the Origins of the American Territorial System," *William and Mary Quarterly*, 3d ser., 29 (1972): 231–62; Jack Ericson Eblen, *The First and Second United States Empires: Governors and Territorial Government, 1784–1912* (Pittsburgh: University of Pittsburgh Press, 1968), chapter 1; Peter S. Onuf, *Statehood and the Union: A History of the Northwest Ordinance* (Bloomington: Indiana University Press, 1987).

3. Manasseh Cutler, *An Explanation of the Map of Federal Lands* (Salem, Mass.: Dabney and Cushing, 1787), 20.

4. The Northwest Territory—the region covered today by the states of Ohio, Indiana, Illinois, Michigan, Wisconsin, and the part of Minnesota east of the Mississippi—acquired its name over a period of time. For most of the first decade of the United States' existence, individual states claimed the lands west of the Appalachians. As Congress gained control of these lands it referred to them as the western territories or the public lands. In 1786, however, Congress issued an ordinance dividing authority for Indian affairs into two departments—the *south-*

ern covered the area south of the Ohio River and the *northern*, the region north of it. The Ordinance of 1787 elaborated on this distinction by referring specifically to the region northwest of the Ohio River. Similarly, in 1790 Congress organized the public lands in the south in an act for "the government of the Territory south of the River Ohio." By the middle of the 1790s the phrase "territory northwest of the Ohio River" had been reversed and abbreviated to the "Northwest Territory."

5. See C. A. Weslager, *The Delaware Indians: A History* (New Brunswick, N. J.: Rutgers University Press, 1972).

6. See Randolph Downes, *Council Fires on the Upper Ohio* (Pittsburgh: University of Pittsburgh Press, 1940); Francis Paul Prucha, *The Great Father: The United States Government and the American Indians*, 2 vols. (Lincoln: University of Nebraska Press, 1984), 1:29–60.

7. Merrill Jensen, *The New Nation: A History of the United States during the Confederation, 1781–1789* (New York: Alfred A. Knopf, 1950); Onuf, "Liberty, Development, and Union."

The most important cessions were those of New York on 1 March 1781; Virginia on 1 March 1784; Massachusetts on 19 April 1785; and Connecticut on 13 September 1786 (excluding the Western Reserve).

8. On the squatters in the Ohio country see Cayton, *Frontier Republic*, chapter 1. On the Clark settlers see Beverley W. Bond, Jr., *The Civilization of the Old Northwest: A Study of Political, Social, and Economic Development, 1788–1812* (New York: Macmillan, 1934), 3.

9. Bond, *Civilization*, 61–66, 294–99; John D. Barnhart and Dorothy L. Riker, *Indiana to 1816: The Colonial Period* (Indianapolis: Indiana Historical Bureau and Indiana Historical Society, 1971), 57–177.

10. See Weslager, *Delaware Indians*; R. David Edmunds, *The Shawnee Prophet* (Lincoln: University of Nebraska Press, 1983), chapter 1.

11. Samuel Holden Parsons to William S. Johnson, 26 November 1785, Manuscripts Division, Library of Congress.

12. Robert F. Berkhofer, Jr., *The White Man's Indian: Images of the American Indian from Columbus to the Present* (New York: Alfred A. Knopf, 1978).

13. Wood, *Rising Glory*, 14–19; McCoy, *Elusive Republic*, 18–22.

14. On the economic growth of the United States in this era see Joyce Appleby, *Capitalism and a New Social Order: The Republican Vision of the 1790s* (New York: New York University Press, 1984); James Henretta, *The Evolution of American Society: An Interdisciplinary Analysis, 1700–1815* (Lexington, Mass.: D. C. Heath, 1973).

15. Steven Hahn and Jonathan Prude, eds., *The Countryside in the Age of Capitalist Transformation: Essays on the Social History of Rural America* (Chapel Hill: University of North Carolina Press, 1985); Thomas M. Doerflinger, *A Vigorous Spirit of Enterprise: Merchants and Economic Development in Revolutionary Philadelphia* (Chapel Hill: University of North Carolina Press for the Institute of Early American History and Culture, 1986); David Brion Davis, *The Problem of Slavery in the Age of Revolution, 1770–1823* (Ithaca, N. Y.: Cornell University Press, 1975).

16. On the Ohio Company of Associates see Cayton, *Frontier Republic*, chapters 2–3.

17. Joseph Doddridge, *Notes on the Settlement and Indian Wars* (Pittsburgh: John S. Ritenour and William T. Lindsey, 1912), 96–101, 109–15; Forrest McDonald and Grady McWhiney, "The Antebellum Southern Herdsman: A Reinterpretation," *Journal of Southern History* 41 (1975): 147–66; Elliott J. Gorn, "'Gouge and Bite, Pull Hair and Scratch': The Social Significance of Fighting in the Southern Backcountry," *American Historical Review* 90 (1985): 18–43.

18. Mary Beth Norton, *Liberty's Daughters: The Revolutionary Experience of American Women, 1750–1800* (Boston: Little, Brown, 1980), esp. 13–15; Anthony F. C. Wallace, *The Death and Rebirth of the Seneca* (New York: Random House, 1969), 28–30. On the family in the eighteenth-century American countryside see James Henretta, "Families and Farms: *Mentalite* in Pre-Industrial America," *William and Mary Quarterly*, 3d ser., 35 (1978): 3–32.

19. "Report of the Proceedings of Winthrop Sargent upon the Land Claims of the Settlers of Vincennes," 31 July 1790, in Clarence E. Carter, ed., *The Territorial Papers of the United States*, 26 vols. (Washington, D.C.: U.S. Government Printing Office, 1934–62), 3:327.

20. "Petition of the Inhabitants of Post Vincennes to Congress," 26 July 1787, in Carter, *Territorial Papers*, 2:58–59.

21. "Petition to Congress from the Illinois Country," 27 August 1787, in Carter, *Territorial Papers*, 2:69.

22. Wallace, *Death and Rebirth of the Seneca*, 24.

23. "Report of the Proceedings of Winthrop Sargent," 31 July 1790, in Carter, *Territorial Papers*, 3:324.

24. Bond, *Civilization*, 327.

25. Gorn, "'Gouge and Bite, Pull Hair and Scratch,'" 27–28, 35–38.

26. Barnhart, *Indiana to 1816*, 178–271.

27. Gorn, "'Gouge and Bite, Pull Hair and Scratch,'" 38–42.

28. Downes, *Council Fires*, 272–75.

29. Arthur Bestor, "Constitutionalism and the Settlement of the West: The Attainment of Consensus, 1754–1784," in John P. Bloom, ed., *The American Territorial System* (Athens: Ohio University Press, 1973), 14–16.

30. Rudolf Freund, "Military Bounty Lands and the Origins of the Public Domain," *Agricultural History* 20 (1946): 8–18.

31. Robert F. Berkhofer, Jr., "The Northwest Ordinance and the Principle of Territorial Evolution," in Bloom, *The American Territorial System*, 47.

32. "Ordinance of April 23, 1784," in Henry Steele Commager, ed., *Documents of American History* (New York: Appleton-Century-Crofts, 1968), 122–23.

33. Eblen, *First and Second United States Empires*, 28–42.

The question of who wrote the Northwest Ordinance has been a matter of much controversy since the nineteenth century. Some writers have argued that the Ordinance of 1787 was merely an elaboration of the Ordinance of 1784, thereby claiming that Thomas Jefferson was the principal author; never mind the facts that Jefferson was in France in 1787 and that the 1784 Ordinance was written by a committee anyway. At various times, other leading candidates have included Rufus King and Nathan Dane, two members of Congress in 1787, and the Rev. Manasseh Cutler, the director of the Ohio Company of Associates, who negotiated that organization's land purchase at the same time the Northwest Ordinance was being approved. Most recent scholars seem to agree that the principal author was probably Virginia Congressman James Monroe, who chaired the committee appointed in 1786 to recommend revisions in territorial policy.

In the end, regardless of who wrote the words, the important point is that the Ordinance was a piece of legislation; almost by definition, therefore, its provisions and language were the work of many minds. Unlike the Declaration of Independence, it was not a general statement of principles with which people could agree or disagree. To identify one person among the numerous members of Congress and its committees as the document's chief author is impossible and unnecessary. For at the bottom, the Northwest Ordinance was simply a thoroughly negotiated reflection of the general sense of many men (in the East) who had debated the nature of American territorial policy throughout the 1780s.

34. "An Ordinance for the government of the territory of the United States North west of the river Ohio," in Carter, *Territorial Papers*, 2:46.

35. Ibid., 45.

36. Ibid., 49.

37. Ibid., 46.

38. Ibid., 47.

39. Ibid., "Report of the Secretary of War to Congress," 10 July 1787, 31.

40. Ibid., 47.

41. Davis, *Problem of Slavery*; Eugene Genovese, *Roll, Jordan, Roll!: The World the Slaves Made* (New York: Pantheon, 1974).

The Vote and the Voters

1. Abraham Yates of New York cast the one negative vote. Why he did it has remained a mystery. Nathan Dane suggested that Yates objected to the slave clause. But, as Jacob Piatt Dunn, Jr., wrote years ago, it could have been anything: "He may have objected to the distinction between lands north and south of the Ohio; he may have objected to the property qualifications of electors and officers; he may have objected to limiting the future states of his section to five. Possibly it was narrowness and stupidity; possibly it was breadth and foresight; possibly some personal interest was interfered with." *Indiana, a Redemption from Slavery*, rev. ed.(Boston: Houghton Mifflin Co., 1905), 215.

2. Merrill Jensen, ed., *The Documentary History of the Ratification of the Constitution*, vol.1, *Constitutional Documents and Records, 1776–1787* (Madison: State Historical Society of Wisconsin, 1976), 187.

3. Richard B. Morris, William Greenleaf, Robert H. Ferrell, *America, a History of the People* (Chicago: Rand McNally and Co., 1971), 1:148.

4. John Porter Bloom, "The Continental Nation—Our Trinity of Revolutionary Testaments," *Western Historical Quarterly* 6 (1975): 14–15, quoted in Phillip R. Shriver, "America's Other Bicentennial," *The Old Northwest* 9 (1983): 228.

5. Phillip R. Shriver observes that the absence of five states called into question even the legitimacy of the act. Ibid.

6. Information on the congressional careers is largely taken from the *Biographical Directory of the American Congress, 1774–1971* (Washington, D.C.: United States Government Printing Office, 1971).

7. Jensen, *Constitutional Documents and Records*, 188 n.7.

8. See, for example, Staughton Lynd, "The Compromise of 1787," in David Curtis Skaggs, ed., *The Old Northwest in the American Revolution, an Anthology* (Madison: The State Historical Society of Wisconsin, 1977), 422.

9. James MacGregor Burns, *The Vineyard of Liberty* (New York: Alfred A. Knopf, 1982), 33.

The Northwest Ordinance: An Annotated Text

1. Clarence E. Carter, ed., *The Territorial Papers of the United States*, 26 vols. (Washington, D.C.: U.S. Government Printing Office, 1934–62), 2:39–50. All further citations from the Ordinance will be from this source.

2. See, for example, the term "ordinance" in T. E. Tomlins, *The Law-Dictionary: Explaining the Rise, Progress, and Present State, of the English law, in Theory and Practice; Defining and Interpreting the Terms or Words of Art; and Comprising Copius Information, Historical, Political, and Commercial, on the Subjects of Our Law, Trade, and Government* (London, 1797).

3. N. Bailey, *A Universal Etymological English Dictionary…The Five-and-Twentieth Edition, carefully enlarged and corrected by Edward Harwood, D.D.* (London, 1790).

4. Henry Campbell Black, *Black's Law Dictionary, Definitions of the Terms and Phrases of American and English Jurisprudence, Ancient and Modern*, 5th ed.(St. Paul, Minn.: West Publishing Co., 1979), 989.

5. On the trend toward primogeniture see William Blackstone, *Commentaries on the Laws of England* (1766), 2:215. See also Theodore F. T. Pluckett, *A Concise History of the Common Law* (London: Butterworth, 1956).

6. For a detailed study of the laws of primogeniture in Virginia see C. Ray Keim, "Primogeniture and Entail in Colonial Virginia," *William and Mary Quarterly*, 3d ser., 25 (1968): 545–86.

7. Jack E. Eblen, "Origins of the American Colonial System," in David Curtis Skaggs, ed., *The Old Northwest in the American Revolution, an Anthology* (Madison: The State Historical Society of Wisconsin, 1977), 465.

8. Phillip R. Shriver, "America's Other Bicentennial," *The Old Northwest* 9 (1983): 227.

9. The territorial officials were appointed by the Confederation Congress until 1789 and thereafter by the president with the consent of Congress.

10. William Henry Smith, ed., *The St. Clair Papers: The Life and Public Services of Arthur St. Clair...with His Correspondence and Other Papers*, 2 vols. (Cincinnati: R. Clarke and Co., 1882), 2:482.

11. Henry Steele Commager, ed., *Documents in American History*, 9th ed., vol. 1, *To 1898* (Englewood Cliffs, N.J.: Prentice-Hall, Inc., 1973), 112–13.

12. Richard H. Kohn, *Eagle and Sword: The Federalists and the Creation of the Military Establishment in America* (New York: Free Press, 1975), 48–53.

13. James Kirby Martin and Mark Edward Lender, *A Respectable Army: The Military Origins of the Republic, 1763–1789* (Arlington Heights, Ill.: Harlan Davidson, Inc., 1982).

14. Commager, *Documents*, 128; Merrill Jensen, *The Documentary History of the Ratification of the Constitution*, vol. 1, *Constitutional Documents and Records, 1786–1787* (Madison: The State Historical Society of Wisconsin, 1976), 61–63; Lawrence Delbert Cress, *Citizens in Arms: The Army and Militia in American Society to the War of 1812* (Chapel Hill: University of North Carolina Press, 1982), 81; Harlow Lindley, Norris F. Schneider, and Milo M. Quaife, *History of the Ordinance of 1787 and the Old Northwest Territory* (Marietta, Ohio: Northwest Territory Celebration Commission, 1937), 21–26.

15. Kohn, *Eagle and Sword*, 74–75; Cress, *Citizens in Arms*, 95–97, 103.

16. Ibid.

17. Commager, *Documents*, 128; Lindley et al., *History of the Ordinance*, 23–27; Jensen, *Constitutional Documents and Records*, 62–63.

18. Kohn, *Eagle and Sword*, 12–35; Cress, *Citizens in Arms*, 78–89.

19. Don E. Fehrenbacher, *The Dred Scott Case: Its Significance in American Law and Politics* (New York: Oxford University Press, 1978), 82, 620 n.25.

20. There do not seem to have been any magistrates, so named in Indiana. See Francis S. Philbrick, ed., *The Laws of Indiana Territory, 1801–1809*, Collections of the Illinois State Historical Library, 21, Law Series, 2 (Springfield: Illinois State Historical Library, 1930; reprint, Indiana Historical Bureau, 1931), 1–32.

21. Robert F. Berkhofer, Jr., "The Northwest Ordinance and the Principle of Territorial Evolution," in John Porter Bloom, ed., *The American Territorial System* (Athens: Ohio University Press, 1973), 48.

22. Computations based on the 1790 census population of 3,929,214.

23. Jack Ericson Eblen, *The First and Second United States Empires: Governors and Territorial Government, 1784–1912* (Pittsburgh: University of Pittsburgh Press, 1968), 110–11 n.38.

24. Theodore C. Pease, ed., *The Laws of the Northwest Territory, 1788–1800*, Collections of the Illinois State Historical Library, 18, Law Series, 1 (Springfield: Illinois State Historical Library, 1925), 4–11.

25. Ibid., 1–4, 12–26; letter of Governor St. Clair to Judges Parsons and Varnum, 21 October 1788, regarding marriage laws, punishment

for crimes, etc., in Carter, *Territorial Papers*, 2:161–62; response by judges to St. Clair, May 1795, in Smith, *St. Clair Papers*, 2:365.

26. Eblen, *First and Second United States Empires*, 87; Jacob Burnet, a member of the territory's legislative council, remarked that the territorial statutes "formed a miserable apology for a code of statute laws." *Notes on the Early Settlement of the North-Western Territory* (Cincinnati: Derby, Bradley and Co., 1847), 304.

27. St. Clair to President Washington, August 1789, in Carter, *Territorial Papers*, 2:206.

28. Eblen, *First and Second United States Empires*, 112. St. Clair rejects the act of original legislation in St. Clair to Judges Parsons and Varnum, 2 August 1788, in Carter, *Territorial Papers*, 3:276. In an early report of Monroe's committee on territorial government, it appears that the governor was to be empowered with the selection of civil laws while the courts were to choose the criminal laws. See Eblen, 34.

29. Eblen, *First and Second United States Empires*, 88–91; Governor St. Clair to Judges Parsons and Varnum, 30 July 1788, in Smith, *St. Clair Papers*, 2:68; St. Clair to Judges Parsons and Varnum, 7 August 1788, in Smith, *St. Clair Papers*, 2:72–73. "When Congress questioned the constitutionality of some of the territory's laws, the governor replied to the effect that unconstitutional laws were better than no laws at all and that to have gone without laws would have produced 'a state of anarchy.'" St. Clair's address to the first territorial legislature, 29 May 1795, in Smith, *St. Clair Papers*, 2:375, quoted in Malcolm J. Rohrbough, *The Trans-Appalachian Frontier: People, Societies, and Institutions, 1775–1850* (New York: Oxford University Press, 1978), 86.

30. Eblen, *First and Second United States Empires*, 88–91; Judges Parsons and Varnum to St. Clair, 31 July 1788, in Smith, *St. Clair Papers*, 2:69–70; Francis S. Philbrick, ed., *The Laws of Illinois Territory, 1809–1818*, Collections of the Illinois State Historical Library, 25, Law Series, 5 (Springfield, Ill.: Illinois State Historical Library, 1950), ccccviii, ccccxv; Beverley W. Bond, Jr., *The Civilization of the Old Northwest* (New York, 1934; reprint ed. New York: AMS Press, 1969), 58–59. For a discussion of the issue of "adoption," see Philbrick, *Laws of Illinois Territory*, cccc-cccciv. Eblen also notes that despite the conflict over the "adoption" issue, none of the governors or judges "received, or even attempted to obtain, an official interpretation from the federal government." Eblen, *First and Second United States Empires*, 91. For a discussion of lawmaking in the Northwest Territory see Eblen, *First and Second United States Empires*, 87–113; St. Clair to President Washington, August 1789, in Carter, *Territorial Papers*, 2:204–12; and Attorney General Levi Lincoln to President Jefferson, 2 February 1802, in Carter, *Territorial Papers*, 3:208–10.

31. Smith, *St. Clair Papers*, 2:457.

32. Peter Onuf, "From Constitution to Higher Law: The Reinterpretation of the Northwest Ordinance," *Ohio History* 94 (1985): 11–12.

33. Julian P. Boyd, ed., *The Papers of Thomas Jefferson*, vol. 6, *1781–*

1784 (Princeton, N.J.: Princeton University Press, 1952), 587–88, 603–607. See also Andrew Cayton's discussion of the Ordinance of 1784 and the Appendix in this volume.

34. *Journals of the Continental Congress, 1774–1789*, 34 vols. (Washington, D.C.: U.S. Government Printing Office, 1904–37), 30:253, 404; Eblen, *First and Second United States Empires*, 30–31, 49–50.

35. See sections seven and eleven of the Ordinance.

36. St. Clair to legislative council, November 1800, in Smith, *St. Clair Papers*, 2:520.

37. Under a 1790 act, justices of the Quarter Sessions courts were allowed to appoint township and certain county officials, divide counties into townships, locate seats of government, define boundaries, and subdivide counties. See Eblen, *First and Second United States Empires*, 119; Bond, *The Civilization of the Old Northwest*, 57–58.

38. William Ewing to Governor St. Clair, 12 July 1800, in Smith, *St. Clair Papers*, 2:496–97. Other petitions are included in ibid., 2:449–50. See also Governor St. Clair to Judge Turner, 2 May 1795, in Carter, *Territorial Papers*, 2:513–14.

39. St. Clair's speech to the legislature, 19 December 1799, in Smith, *St. Clair Papers*, 2:476–77; St. Clair to justices of Adams County, 29 June 1798, in Smith, *St. Clair Papers*, 2:426; Eblen, *First and Second United States Empires*, 126.

40. Smith, *St. Clair Papers*, 2:477–79, 515–16; Eblen, *First and Second United States Empires*, 181. St. Clair's actions provoked a remonstrance against the absolute veto power granted to the governor. According to Jacob Burnet, St. Clair intimated "a want of confidence in the judgment and discretion of the Assembly, in deciding when the number of inhabitants, or the situation of a district, rendered it necessary, or proper, to alter or divide it, and thereby establish a new county; and, as if anxious to make his power more sensibly felt, he proceeded, immediately, to create and organise new counties, out of old ones, varying somewhat from the plan adopted by the Assembly; and to establish them by proclamation, without consulting the Legislature." Burnet, *Early Settlement*, 376. Burnet also notes that the legislature insisted that "after the Governor had laid out the country into counties and townships, as he had already done, under the first grade of Government, it was competent for them to pass laws, altering, dividing, and multiplying, them at their pleasure, to be submitted to the Governor for his approbation [and that] when the Territory had been divided into counties by the Governor, his exclusive power was exhausted, and any alterations thereafter required, were to be made by the Legislature, with his assent" (321).

41. Smith, *St. Clair Papers*, 2:518. St. Clair's words are mandatory in nature and indicate that county-making is purely an executive act and duty.

42. Attorney General Levi Lincoln to President Jefferson, 2 February 1802, in Carter, *Territorial Papers*, 3:208–11.

43. Thomas Worthington to secretary of treasury, August 1801, in ibid., 3:171–72.

44. Opposition to St. Clair was organized by Nathaniel Massie and Thomas Worthington, who charged in an 1802 letter to James Madison that St. Clair "has violated the constitution of this Territory in assuming to himself the legislative powers thereof, by erecting new counties out of counties already laid out, and thereby altering their boundaries, and fixing the permanent seat of justice." Smith, *St. Clair Papers*, 2:564.

45. Both Eblen and G. L. Wilson ("Arthur St. Clair and the Administration of the Old Northwest, 1788–1802," Ph.D. dissertation, University of Southern California, 1957) contend that St. Clair resisted the creation of new counties in order to assure Federalist control in the territory, thereby minimizing the power of the emerging Jeffersonian Republicans. For a discussion of the conflict over county-making powers see Eblen, *The First and Second United States Empires*, 182; Bond, *Civilization of the Old Northwest*, 92–99, 104–107; Burnet, *Early Settlement*, 375–79; Secretary of State Madison to St. Clair, 23 June 1802, in Carter, *Territorial Papers*, 3:231. For a list of accusations and charges against St. Clair see Smith, *St. Clair Papers*, 2:563–70.

46. "The Proclamation of 1763," in Commager, *Documents*, 47–50.

47. *Journals of the Continental Congress*, 2:195–99, 25:602.

48. *Indiana Senate Journal*, 1826–27, 7–8, 10; George Pence and Nellie C. Armstrong, *Indiana Boundaries: Territory, State, and County* (Indianapolis: Indiana Historical Bureau, 1933), 47. During the 1832–33 session, forty-three Miami County residents petitioned for county organization, but their pleas went unheeded since half of the proposed county still belonged to the Miami Indians. *Senate Journal*, 1832–33, 61–62.

49. Pence and Armstrong, *Indiana Boundaries*, 55. Indiana counties that encroached upon Indian lands included LaPorte, 1832; Miami, 1832; an extension of Randolph, 1820; Tippecanoe, 1826; and Wabash, 1832.

50. Although Article Six of the Ordinance expressly prohibited slavery in the Northwest Territory, the words "free inhabitants" were used at several places in the document. For a discussion of this contradiction see Charles Kettleborough, *Constitution Making in Indiana*, 2 vols. (Indianapolis: Indiana Historical Bureau, 1916), 1:27 n.17.

51. The act of Congress of 7 May 1800, organizing Indiana Territory, introduced a change regarding the advance to the second stage. Instead of waiting until the free adult male population reached 5,000, the second stage could be instituted whenever the governor was given "satisfactory evidence" that a majority of freeholders (voters) favored the change. Kettleborough, *Constitution Making*, 1:42.

52. The act of 1800 stipulated that until the free adult male population reached 5,000, the number of representatives should not be less than seven or more than nine, to be apportioned by the governor among the counties according to population. This arrangement remained in force until Congress, by an act of 27 February 1809, authorized the general assembly to apportion the membership of the lower house and limit the number of representatives to a maximum of twelve

and a minimum of nine. When the free adult white male population reached 6,000, the number of representatives was to be regulated by the terms of the Ordinance. Kettleborough, *Constitution Making*, 1:42, 57.

53. In response to complaints from the territorial legislature, Congress passed an act on 3 March 1811, making appointees of the governor (justices of the peace and militia officers excepted) ineligible to serve in the general assembly. Kettleborough, *Constitution Making*, 1:58–59.

54. Chilton Williamson, *American Suffrage: From Property to Democracy, 1760–1860* (Princeton, N.J.: Princeton University Press, 1960), 135.

55. An act of Congress of 26 February 1808 extended slightly the right of suffrage. Aside from being a free adult white male, a citizen of the United States, and a resident of Indiana Territory one year, an inhabitant could vote if he (1) owned fifty acres of land, (2) was purchasing fifty acres of land, or (3) owned a town lot valued at $100. All property qualifications were removed by Congress in an act of 3 March 1811. It gave the vote to all free adult white males who paid any kind of tax and had resided in the territory for one year. Kettleborough, *Constitution Making*, 1:48, 58.

56. After the adoption of the Constitution, Congress in 1789 authorized the president of the United States, with the advice and consent of the Senate, to appoint and remove territorial officers. Ibid., 1:36–37.

57. Congress gradually democratized the process by which the legislative councilors were chosen. An act of 27 February 1809 authorized the qualified voters of the territory to elect members of the legislative council. The governor was to divide the territory into districts for the purposes of election. In December of the same year Congress provided that vacancies in the council were to be filled by a special election called by the governor. The act of 3 March 1811, making appointees of the governor ineligible to serve in the general assembly, applied to councilors as well as to representatives. Finally, by an act of 3 March 1814, Congress authorized the house of representatives to apportion the territory for the election of legislative councilors. Kettleborough, *Constitution Making*, 1:56–60.

58. The United States Constitution after 1789.

59. For an example of contemporary forms of an oath and an affirmation see the Vermont Constitution of 1786 in William F. Swindler, ed., *Sources and Documents of United States Constitutions*, 10 vols. (Dobbs Ferry, N.Y.: Oceanic Publications, Inc., 1979), 9:503.

60. This brief discussion of territorial representation is largely taken from Jo Tice Bloom, "Early Delegates in the House of Representatives," in Bloom, *The American Territorial System*, 65–76.

61. *Papers of the Continental Congress*, no. 30, fol. 101; *Journals of the Continental Congress*, 26:278.

62. Jay A. Barrett, *Evolution of the Ordinance of 1787, with an Account of the Earlier Plans for the Government of the Northwest Territory* (New York: G.P. Putnam's Sons, 1891), 68–69.

63. *Journals of the Continental Congress*, 30:67–68, 251–55.

64. Carter, *Territorial Papers*, 2:46 n.24.
65. Barrett, *Evolution of the Ordinance*, 11.
66. Anson Phelps Stokes and Leo Pfeffer, *Church and State in the United States* (New York: Harper and Row, 1964), 155. See also Henry Steele Commager, "The Significance of Religion in American History," in Henry B. Clark, ed., *Freedom of Religion in America: Historical Roots, Philosophical Concepts, and Contemporary Problems* (New Brunswick, N. J.: Rutgers University Press, 1982), 19–20.
67. William Warren Sweet, "The American Colonial Environment and Religious Liberty," *Church History* 4 (1935): 45, 51–54; Commager, "Significance of Religion," 14–16. See also Loren P. Beth, *The American Theory of Church and State* (Gainesville: University of Florida Press, 1958), 58–59; Stokes and Pfeffer, *Church and State in the United States*, 21.
68. Writings on the development of religious liberty in the colonies are voluminous. For solid brief accounts, see Stokes and Pfeffer, *Church and State in the United States*; Stanford H. Cobb, *The Rise of Religious Liberty in America: A History* (New York: Macmillan, 1902). On Roger Williams see Beth, *American Theory of Church and State*, 11–12, 53–54; Evarts B. Greene, *Religion and the State: The Making and Testing of an American Tradition* (Ithaca, N. Y.: Cornell University Press, 1941), 47–59.
69. Conrad Moehlman, *The American Constitutions and Religion: Religious References in the Charters of the Thirteen Colonies and the Constitutions of the Forty-Eight States* (Berne, Ind.; n.p., 1938), 12. On the direct influence of Locke upon Jefferson and others see Jefferson's "Notes on Locke and Shaftesbury" in Boyd, *Papers of Thomas Jefferson*, 1:545; Dumas Malone, *Jefferson the Virginian* (Boston: Little, Brown and Co., 1948), 275–76; S. Gerald Sandler, "Lockean Ideas in Thomas Jefferson's *Bill for Establishing Religious Freedom*," *Journal of the History of Ideas* 21 (1960): 110–16; Sanford Kessler, "Locke's Influence on Jefferson's 'Bill for Establishing Religious Freedom,'" *Journal of Church and State* 25 (1983): 231–52. Interestingly, the cause of religious liberty increasingly entered into United States' foreign relations during this period. Two treaties of the 1780s, with the Netherlands and Portugal, included specific provisions for religious freedom, and American concern over the Quebec Act of 1774 was couched in the rhetoric of freedom of conscience. See Boyd, *Papers of Thomas Jefferson*, 9:415; Stokes and Pfeffer, *Church and State in the United States*, 31–32, 84–85.
70. Stokes and Pfeffer, *Church and State in the United States*, 65. See also 65–71 and, for comparable struggles in other states, 71–82.
71. Boyd, *Papers of Thomas Jefferson*, 1:344, 353, 363.
72. Ibid., 2:545–46. See also Malone, *Jefferson the Virginian*, 274–80.
73. William T. Hutchinson, et al., eds., *The Papers of James Madison*, 10 vols. (Chicago: University of Chicago Press, 1962–1977), 1:170–71 (italics mine). See also Gaillard Hunt, "James Madison and Religious Liberty," *Annual Report of the American Historical Association for the Year 1901*, 2 vols. (Washington: U.S. Government Printing Office, 1902), 1:166–67.
74. Hutchinson, et al., *Papers of James Madison*, 8:299. For accounts of

the dramatic events surrounding this incident in Virginia's struggle for religious liberty, see ibid., 8:295–302; Stokes and Pfeffer, *Church and State in the United States*, 55–69; Forrest McDonald, *Novus Ordo Seclorum: The Intellectual Origins of the Constitution* (Lawrence: University of Kansas, 1985), 44–45.

75. Carter, *Territorial Papers*, 2:46; Arthur Bestor, "Constitutionalism and the Settlement of the West: The Attainment of Consensus, 1754–1784," in Bloom, *The American Territorial System*, 32–33; Barrett, *Evolution of the Ordinance*, 60–61. Some early interpreters of the Ordinance pointed directly to the Declaration of Rights in the Massachusetts Constitution of 1780 as the model for Article One. Proponents of this theory saw Nathan Dane and Manasseh Cutler as the primary forces at work in the writing of the Ordinance. See Barrett, *Evolution of the Ordinance*, 60; William F. Poole, *The Ordinance of 1787, and Dr. Manasseh Cutler as an Agent in its Formation* (Cambridge, Mass.: Welch, Bigelow, and Company, 1876), 32–35.

76. Stokes and Pfeffer, *Church and State in the United States*, 19, 85; Boyd, *Papers of Thomas Jefferson*, 2:546, 9:415.

77. Lee to Washington, 15 July 1787, in Edmund C. Burnett, ed., *Letters of Members of the Continental Congress*, 8 vols. (Washington: Carnegie Institute, 1921–36), 8:620. See also Berkhofer, "The Northwest Ordinance and the Principle of Territorial Evolution," in Bloom, *The American Territorial System*, 49–52.

78. The starting point for any study of the actions of Congress has for many years been Edmund C. Burnett's *Letters of Members of the Continental Congress*. This work is now being superseded by an enlarged and updated edition, but the relevant volumes for the late 1780s have not yet appeared. The correspondence dealing with 1786 and 1787 appears in volume 8, particularly pages 374–82 and 609–62. More specifically, see James Monroe to James Madison, 3 September 1786, 460–62, on the topic of union, and Edward Carrington to Thomas Jefferson, 23 October 1787, 8:660–62, on the idea of empire. For the role of diplomacy see Rufus King to Elbridge Gerry, 4 June 1786, 8:380–82. On economic and land policy note Edward Carrington to James Madison, 25 July 1787, 8:628, and Richard Henry Lee to Francis Lightfoot Lee, 14 July 1787, 8:619–20. The role of the Ohio Company in authorship is noted in Nathan Dane to Rufus King, 16 July 1787, 8:621–22.

Several works by modern historians seek to place these issues in context. The rhetoric of Union and empire is explored in Peter S. Onuf, "Liberty, Development, and Union: Visions of the West in the 1780s," *William and Mary Quarterly*, 3d ser., 43 (1986): 179–213. The tangled problems of public finance are explained well in E. James Ferguson, *The Power of the Purse* (Chapel Hill: University of North Carolina Press, 1961). The background of land policy is summarized in George W. Geib, "The Land Ordinance of 1785: A Bicentennial Review," *Indiana Magazine of History* 81 (1985): 1–13. Reginald Horsman, *The Frontier in the Formative Years, 1783–1815* (New York: Holt, Reinhart and Winston, 1970) offers a good overview of the era.

79. The Northwest Ordinance was adopted by the Confederation

Congress. The "delegates" referred to are the existing states' representatives to this Confederation Congress, not delegates from a prospective state.

80. Carter, *Territorial Papers*, 2:6–9, quotation, 7.

81. Barrett, *Evolution of the Ordinance*, 17–27, and the maps following pages 16 and 24; *Journals of the American Congress*, 4 vols. (Washington, D.C., 1823), 4:378–80; *Journals of the Continental Congress*, 26:118–20.

82. Barrett, *Evolution of the Ordinance*, 33–35; Monroe to Thomas Jefferson, 19 January 1786, in Stanislaus Murray Hamilton, *The Writings of James Monroe*, 7 vols. (New York: Putnam, 1898–1903), 1:117–18.

83. The argument in favor of reducing the number of states to be created out of the northwestern lands, including the point that "due attention ought to be paid to natural boundaries" when fixing these states' borders, is expressed succinctly in *Journals of the American Congress*, 4:663.

84. Carter, *Territorial Papers*, 2:172–73.

85. On the state boundaries and their departure from the line prescribed by the Northwest Ordinance, see Mrs. Frank J. Sheehan, *The Northern Boundary of Indiana* (Indiana Historical Society *Publications*, vol. 8, no. 6, Indianapolis: Indiana Historical Society, 1928), 293–96; Solon J. Buck, *Illinois in 1818* (Springfield, Ill.: Illinois Centennial Commission, 1917), 221–22, 224–25; R. Carlyle Buley, *The Old Northwest: Pioneer Period, 1815–1840*, 2 vols. (Indianapolis: Indiana Historical Society, 1950), 2:190–203, especially the citations in footnote 122.

86. *Journals of the American Congress*, 4:380. The least populous state during the period was Delaware, with a population estimated at 45,000 in 1780. *Historical Statistics of the United States: Colonial Times to 1970*, 2 vols. (Washington, D.C., 1975) 2:1168.

87. Barrett, *Evolution of the Ordinance*, 42–43. The 200,000 figure is calculated based upon the estimated populations of the thirteen original states as of 1780; see *Historical Statistics of the United States*, 2:1168.

88. Barrett, *Evolution of the Ordinance*, 67. Illinois, for example, was admitted to the Union based on a census showing a population of only 40,258—and even that figure was probably inflated. Clarence W. Alvord, *The Illinois Country, 1673–1818* (Springfield: Illinois Centennial Commission, 1920), 459–62; Buck, *Illinois in 1818*, 213, 219, 221, 227, 238–41, 263–65.

89. Robert Berkhofer, "The Ordinance of 1784," in Skaggs, *The Old Northwest in the American Revolution*, 408.

90. David Griffin, "Historians and the Sixth Article of the Ordinance of 1787," *Ohio History* 78 (1969): 252.

91. Ibid., 252–60.

92. Staughton Lynd, "The Compromise of 1787," in Skaggs, *The Old Northwest in the American Revolution*, 420–40.

93. Emma Lou Thornbrough, *The Negro in Indiana before 1900: A Study of a Minority* (Indianapolis: Indiana Historical Bureau, 1957), 6–8.

94. Ibid., 8–9; Philbrick, *The Laws of Indiana Territory*, 42–43. The efforts to legalize slavery are discussed in detail in Jacob Piatt Dunn, Jr., *Indiana, a Redemption from Slavery*, rev. ed. (Boston: Houghton Miff-

lin, 1905). Most of the papers connected therewith are reproduced in Dunn, ed., *Slavery Petitions and Papers* (Indiana Historical Society *Publications*, vol. 2, no. 12, Indianapolis: Indiana Historical Society, 1894).

95. Thornbrough, *Negro in Indiana*, 9–12.

96. Ibid., 13–16, 22.

97. Ibid., 23.

98. Ibid., 25–26; State v. Lasselle, 1 Blackford (Ind.), 61–62.

99. Thornbrough, *Negro in Indiana*, 27–30; Mary a Woman of Color, 1 Blackford (Ind.), 125–26.

Putting the Ordinance to Work in the Northwest

1. Edmund C. Burnett, *The Continental Congress* (New York: Macmillan, 1941), 680–87; Merrill Jensen, *The New Nation: A History of the United States during the Confederation* (New York: Alfred A. Knopf, 1950), 357–59; Robert F. Berkhofer, Jr., "The Northwest Ordinance and the Principle of Territorial Evolution," in John P. Bloom, ed., *The American Territorial System* (Athens, Ohio: Ohio University Press, 1973), 45–55.

2. Burnett, *Continental Congress*, 686–87; *Journals of the Continental Congress, 1774–1789*, 34 vols. (Washington, D.C.: U.S. Government Printing Office, 1904–1937), 33:599–602, 610, 698–700; William Henry Smith, ed., *The St. Clair Papers: The Life and Public Services of Arthur St. Clair*, 2 vols. (Cincinnati: Robert Clarke and Co., 1882), 1:126–36; "Manasseh Cutler," in Clifford K. Shipton, *Sibley's Harvard Graduates*, vol. 16, *Biographical Sketches of Those Who Attended Harvard College in the Classes of 1764–1767* (Boston: Massachusetts Historical Society, 1972), 138–54; Lee N. Newcomer, "Manasseh Cutler's Writings: A Note on Editorial Practice," *Mississippi Valley Historical Review* 47 (1960): 88–101.

3. Arthur St. Clair, *A Narrative of the Manner in Which the Campaign against . . . the Indians Was Conducted* (Philadelphia: Jane Aitken, 1812), 32; Patrick J. Furlong, "The Investigation of General Arthur St. Clair, 1792–1793," *Capitol Studies* 5 (1977): 81–82.

4. Burnett, *Continental Congress*, 687–88; *Journals of the Continental Congress*, 33:599–602, 698–700. While the governor was appointed for three years, the secretary's term was four years, and the judges served during good behavior and were paid $800 a year. For Sargent's career see Shipton, *Biographical Sketches*, 17:614–26; for Symmes see the sketch by Beverley W. Bond, Jr., in *Dictionary of American Biography*, 18:258–59.

5. *Journals of the Continental Congress*, 33:698–700; commissions for the governor and the secretary were approved by Congress on 23 October, and they were to assume their offices on 1 February 1788. See also Clarence E. Carter, ed., *Territorial Papers of the United States*, 26 vols. (Washington, D.C.: U.S. Government Printing Office, 1934–62), 2:78–88.

6. Harmar to Knox, 24 November, 9 December 1787, 10 January, 15 June 1788; Harmar to St. Clair, 25 November 1787; St. Clair to Knox, 27 January, 14 March, 23 June, 5, 13 July 1788; Richard Butler to St. Clair, 1, 14 July 1788; St. Clair to Butler, 15 July 1788; all in Smith, *St. Clair Papers*, 2:30–53. See also St. Clair to Knox, 27 January, 5, 13, 16 July 1788; Sargent to St. Clair, 17 February 1788, and the correspondence and

petitions regarding land claims at Vincennes, all in Carter, *Territorial Papers*, 2:89–132.

7. For the governor's speech and the formal reply see Smith, *St. Clair Papers*, 2:53–57; another formal reply may be found in Carter, *Territorial Papers*, 2:132–33.

8. St. Clair to Knox, 16 July 1788; St. Clair to Washington, 11 June 1790; Symmes and George Turner to St. Clair, 6 October 1790; Smith, *St. Clair Papers*, 2:58, 179, 187–88; St. Clair and Sargent both complained that their salaries did not cover their official and personal expenses, particularly for their required travels through the vast territory; see St. Clair to Jefferson, 19 March 1790; Sargent to Washington, 1 August 1790; Sargent to Timothy Pickering, 20 June 1796; Carter, *Territorial Papers*, 2:231, 295–96, 560. For the changes in the Ordinance see "An Act to Provide for the Government of the Territory North-west of the river Ohio," 1 Statutes at Large 50, adopted 7 August 1789.

9. St. Clair to Knox, 14 June 1789, 1 May 1790; Pierre Gibault to St. Clair, 9 June 1790; St. Clair to Washington, 11 June 1790; Smith, *St. Clair Papers*, 2:115–21, 129, 136–42 (quotations), 148–49, 179–80 and passim; for further documents on the Vincennes land claims see Carter, *Territorial Papers*, 2:145–50, 189–282.

10. The official record from Sargent's Journal of the Executive Proceedings of the Territory appears in Carter, *Territorial Papers*, 3:278–79, 294–95, 301–303, 313–14. On the importance of county government see Malcolm J. Rohrbough, *The Trans-Appalachian Frontier: People, Societies, and Institutions, 1775–1850* (New York: Oxford University Press, 1978), 119–22.

11. St. Clair reviewed the long dispute in letters to Joshua Coit, 24 December 1794, and to Symmes, 28 April 1795; see also Symmes to St. Clair, 26 March 1795; Smith, *St. Clair Papers*, 2:333–48. For the governor's speech to the judges at the legislative session and the results of their deliberations, see ibid., 353–71.

12. St. Clair to Edmund Randolph, 4 May 1795; Randolph to Tench Coxe, 1 June; Bradford to Wolcott, 19 June; Wolcott to St. Clair, 20 June; St. Clair to Wolcott, 24 July; Carter, *Territorial Papers*, 2:514–24.

13. There is no good modern account of the tangled land claims and purchases in the Northwest Territory. The subject is covered in broad terms by Rohrbough, *Trans-Appalachian Frontier*, 64–81. The beginning of the Ohio Company is described by Rudolf Freund, "Military Bounty Lands and the Origins of the Public Domain," *Agricultural History* 20 (1946): 8–18, reprinted in Harry N. Schreiber, ed., *The Old Northwest: Studies in Regional History, 1787–1910* (Lincoln: University of Nebraska Press, 1969), 6–27. For the French letters see Smith, *St. Clair Papers*, 2:152–54; for St. Clair's letter to the French residents of Gallipolis, 21 November, and his report to Knox, 26 November 1790, see ibid., 190–91, 195; additional documents on the subject may be found in Carter, *Territorial Papers*, 2:311, 337, 417–28, 450–51, 462–70, 598–601.

14. Bond, "Symmes"; St. Clair to Alexander Hamilton, 25 May 1791; St. Clair to Timothy Pickering, July 1799; St. Clair to the House of Representatives, 16 October 1799; St. Clair to John Ross, December

1799; St. Clair's address to the territorial legislature, 5 November 1800, 26 November 1801, legislative instructions to Paul Fearing, December 1801; Smith, *St. Clair Papers*, 2:209–13, 443–45, 465–71, 480–81, 507–509, 536–37, 545–47; Symmes to St. Clair, 23 May 1791; St. Clair to Hamilton, 25 May 1791; Jefferson to St. Clair, and to Symmes, both 6 August 1791; Carter, *Territorial Papers*, 2:343–50; Act of Congress of 12 April 1792, and list of other documents about the Symmes Purchase, ibid., 388–94, 490–98; St. Clair to Symmes, 12, 14 July 1791, and proclamations by the governor, 19 July, 15 September 1791; ibid., 3:350–58. Judge Putnam was also deeply involved in land speculations which sometimes came before his court, St. Clair to Jefferson, 24 December 1794, Smith, *St. Clair Papers*, 2:333–34.

15. *Journals of the Continental Congress*, 33:599–602. St. Clair was not to assume the Indian superintendency from Richard Butler until 14 August 1788, although the appointment was made ten months earlier. A good introduction to the complex story of Indian relations appears in Dwight L. Smith, "Provocation and Occurrence of Indian-White Warfare in the Early American Period in the Old Northwest," *Northwest Ohio Quarterly* 33 (1961): 132–47.

16. For the campaign see St. Clair's own account in defense of his actions, *Narrative of the Manner in Which the Campaign against the Indians . . . Was Conducted*; modern studies start with James R. Jacobs, *The Beginning of the U.S. Army, 1783–1812* (Princeton, N. J.: Princeton University Press, 1947), 66–123; more recent interpretations are offered by Richard H. Kohn, *Eagle and Sword: The Federalists and the Creation of the Military Establishment in America, 1783–1802* (New York: Free Press, 1975), 107–16; and Francis P. Prucha, *The Sword of the Republic: The United States Army on the Frontier, 1783–1846* (New York: Macmillan, 1969), 20–29; for the congressional investigation of St. Clair see Furlong, "The Investigation of General Arthur St. Clair"; for Sargent's journal see Carter, *Territorial Papers*, 3:334–59.

17. For Wayne's campaign see the military histories cited above and also Paul D. Nelson, *Anthony Wayne: Soldier of the Early Republic* (Bloomington: Indiana University Press, 1985); for the growth of a secure and stable territorial society see Rohrbough, *The Trans-Appalachian Frontier*, 64–87, 115–21. Beverley W. Bond., Jr., *The Civilization of the Old Northwest: A Study of Political, Social, and Economic Development, 1788–1812* (New York: Macmillan, 1934), is an older work of lasting value. On the political tensions after 1795 see Peter S. Onuf, "From Constitution to Higher Law: The Reinterpretation of the Northwest Ordinance," *Ohio History* 94 (1985): 6–14, and Jeffrey P. Brown, "Timothy Pickering and the Northwest Territory," *Northwest Ohio Quarterly* 53 (1981): 119–26.

18. For the population estimates see Carter, *Territorial Papers*, 2:470, 649; for Chillicothe and the Western Reserve, John D. Barnhart, *Valley of Democracy: The Frontier Versus the Plantation in the Ohio Valley 1775–1818* (Bloomington: Indiana University Press, 1953), 140–41, and Smith, *St. Clair Papers*, 1:215–16; see also St. Clair to Massie, 29 June, 23 July 1798, ibid., 425–31 and passim. See also Alfred B. Sears, *Thomas Worthington:*

Father of Ohio Statehood (Columbus: Ohio State University Press, for the Ohio Historical Society, 1958), 13–48.

19. Smith, *St. Clair Papers*, 1:196–97, 207–208; Barnhart, *Valley of Democracy*, 139–41; for popular demands for an assembly see also Sargent to Pickering, 30 September 1796, 5, 14 August 1797, Carter, *Territorial Papers*, 2:578, 618–19, 622–24.

20. Sargent to Pickering, 9, 20 June, 9 August 1796; Sargent to St. Clair, 20, 30 September, 1 December 1796, Carter, *Territorial Papers*, 2:558–64, 573–76. St. Clair to Sargent, 13, 28 August, 6 September 1796, Smith, *St. Clair Papers*, 2:404–406, 413–17. Sargent's memorandum listing St. Clair's absences appears in Carter, *Territorial Papers*, 2:647–48.

21. Sargent to Pickering, 30 September 1796, Carter, *Territorial Papers*, 2:579; St. Clair to Pickering, 1 July 1799, ibid., 3:27; for the establishment of the representative stage see ibid., 514–15 and Smith, *St. Clair Papers*, 1:208.

22. Smith, *St. Clair Papers*, 1:208–209; Barnhart, *Valley of Democracy*, 147–49; Sears, *Worthington*, 48–54; for the governor's opening address to the representatives, Smith, *St. Clair Papers*, 2:438–40.

23. Smith, *St. Clair Papers*, 1:209–14; the governor's address and the responses of both houses appear in ibid., 2:446–62; Dorothy B. Goebel, *William Henry Harrison: A Political Biography* (Indianapolis: Indiana Historical Bureau, 1926), 37–43; Freeman Cleaves, *Old Tippecanoe: William Henry Harrison and His Time* (New York: C. Scribner's Sons, 1939), 22–29.

24. Smith, *St. Clair Papers*, 1:213–14; the record of laws passed is outlined in ibid., 2:447–53; see also Barnhart, *Valley of Democracy*, 148–49, and Sears, *Worthington*, 54–63.

25. Barnhart, *Valley of Democracy*, 149–52; Bond, *Civilization of the Old Northwest*, 100–102; Smith, *St. Clair Papers*, 1:217–22; Carter, *Territorial Papers*, 3:86–88; John D. Barnhart and Dorothy L. Riker, *Indiana to 1816: The Colonial Period* (Indianapolis: Indiana Historical Bureau and Indiana Historical Society, 1971), 310–13; Cleaves, *Old Tippecanoe*, 29–32; Goebel, *Harrison*, 44–51; Sears, *Worthington*, 68–72.

26. Smith, *St. Clair Papers*, 1:217–23; Randolph C. Downes, *Frontier Ohio, 1788–1803* (Columbus: Ohio Historical Society, 1935), passim; Sears, *Worthington*, 54–72; Bond, *Civilization of the Old Northwest*, 106–12.

27. Bond, *Civilization of the Old Northwest*, 102–104; Sears, *Worthington*, 56–60; the governor's address appears in Smith, *St. Clair Papers*, 2:501–10.

28. Bond, *Civilization of the Old Northwest*, 104–108; for the governor's address and the assembly's replies see Smith, *St. Clair Papers*, 2:501–16; for the assembly's letter to the people about statehood, ibid., 524–25; for the governor's reappointment, John Brown to St. Clair, 24 December 1800 and 29 January 1801; also James Ross to St. Clair, 3 February 1801, ibid., 526–30; and also Sears, *Worthington*, 58–63.

29. Sears, *Worthington*, 68–71; Jacob Burnet, *Notes on the Early Settlement of the North-Western Territory* (Cincinnati: Derby, Bradley and Co., 1847), 328–35. The entire controversy is well described by Ran-

dolph C. Downes, "The Statehood Contest in Ohio," *Mississippi Valley Historical Review* 18 (1931): 155–71.

30. Bond, *Civilization of the Old Northwest*, 108–16; Sears, *Worthington*, 73–88; Burnet, *Early Settlement*, 335–49. The governor's address and the replies from the assembly may be found in Smith, *St. Clair Papers*, 2:534–40, and the bill for division of the territory and the resulting dispute, in ibid., 543–51; see also Massie to Worthington, 3 January 1802, and Tiffin to Worthington, 8 January, ibid., 552–54.

31. St. Clair's speech is in Smith, *St. Clair Papers*, 2:592–97; the accusations against him may be followed in Worthington to Jefferson, 30 January 1802; Massie to Madison, [February, undated]; Tiffin to Worthington, 1 February; Massie to Worthington, 8 February; George Tod to Madison, 29 May; with the governor's defense in St. Clair to Jefferson, 13 February, all in ibid., 563–85. See also Bond, *Civilization of the Old Northwest*, 116–19.

32. Madison to St. Clair, 22 November 1802, Carter, *Territorial Papers*, 3:260; St. Clair to Madison, 21 December 1802, Smith, *St. Clair Papers*, 2:599–601. See also Worthington to Jefferson, 8 November 1802, to Albert Gallatin, 17 November, and to William B. Giles, 17 November, as well as Gallatin to Jefferson, 20 November, all in Carter, *Territorial Papers*, 3:254–59. These events are well described by Bond, *Civilization of the Old Northwest*, 118–19, 131, and by Sears, *Worthington*, 86–98. St. Clair's policies and character are defended by Burnet, *Early Settlement*, 335–83.

33. Barnhart, *Valley of Democracy*, 154–60; Sears, *Worthington*, 88–107.

34. For Indiana the best survey is Barnhart, *Valley of Democracy*, 161–96, and for greater detail, Barnhart and Riker, *Indiana to 1816*, 314–69, 412–63. See also Goebel, *Harrison*, 53–107, and Cleaves, *Old Tippecanoe*, 33–68.

35. Barnhart, *Valley of Democracy*, 197–215 (quotations at 203); Robert P. Howard, *Illinois: A History of the Prairie State* (Grand Rapids: Eerdmans Publishing Co., 1972), 76–79, 98–104.

36. Alec R. Gilpin, *The Territory of Michigan* (East Lansing: Michigan State University Press, 1970), covers the tangled story of Michigan's long territorial period in scholarly fashion.

37. Moses M. Strong, *History of the Wisconsin Territory, from 1836 to 1848* (Madison: Democratic Printing Co., state printers, 1885).

Appendix

1. Julian P. Boyd, ed., *The Papers of Thomas Jefferson*, vol. 6, *1781–1784* (Princeton, N. J.: Princeton University Press, 1950), 613–15.

Selected Bibliography

Abernethy, Thomas P. *Western Lands and the American Revolution.* New York: Appleton-Century Co., 1937.

Alden, George H. "The Evolution of the American System of Forming and Admitting New States into the Union." *Annals of the American Academy of Political and Social Science* 18 (1901): 469–79.

Barnhart, John D. *Valley of Democracy: The Frontier Versus the Plantation in the Ohio Valley, 1775–1818.* Bloomington: Indiana University Press, 1953.

Barnhart, John D., and Riker, Dorothy L. *Indiana to 1816: The Colonial Period.* Indianapolis: Indiana Historical Bureau and Indiana Historical Society, 1971.

Barnhart, Terry A.; Cole, Charles C., Jr.; and Williamsen, Patricia N. *Discussion Guide for the Northwest Ordinance.* Columbus, Ohio: Ohio Humanities Council, 1985.

Barrett, Jay A. *Evolution of the Ordinance of 1787 with an Account of the Earlier Plans for the Government of the Northwest Territory.* New York: G. P. Putnam's Sons, 1891.

Bartlett, Richard A. *The New Country: A Social History of the American Frontier, 1776–1890.* New York: Oxford University Press, 1974.

Bayard, Charles J. "The Development of the Public Land Policy, 1783–1820, with Special Reference to Indiana." Ph.D. dissertation, Indiana University, 1956.

Berkhofer, Robert F., Jr. "Jefferson, the Ordinance of 1784, and the Origins of the American Territorial System." *William and Mary Quarterly*, 3d ser., 29 (1972): 231–62.

————. "The Northwest Ordinance and the Principle of Territorial Evolution." In *The American Territorial System*, edited by John Porter Bloom. Athens, Ohio: Ohio University Press, 1973.

Billington, Ray Allen. "The Historians of the Northwest Ordinance." Illinois State Historical Society *Journal* 40 (1947): 347–413.

Bloom, John Porter. "The Continental Nation—Our Trinity of Revolutionary Testaments." *Western Historical Quarterly* 6 (1975): 5–15.

————, ed. *The American Territorial System*. National Archives Conferences, vol. 5. Athens, Ohio: Ohio University Press, 1973.

Bond, Beverley W., Jr. "An American Experiment in Colonial Government." *Mississippi Valley Historical Review* 15 (1928): 221–35.

Burnett, Edmund C. *Letters of Members of the Continental Congress*. 8 vols. Washington, D.C.: Carnegie Institute, 1921-36.

Carter, Clarence E., ed. *The Territorial Papers of the United States*. Vols. 2–3. Washington, D.C.: Government Printing Office, 1934.

Cayton, Andrew R. L. *The Frontier Republic: Ideology and Politics in the Ohio Country, 1780–1825*. Kent, Ohio: Kent University Press, 1986.

Coles, Edward. *History of the Ordinance of 1787*. Philadelphia, 1856.

————. " 'A Quiet Independence': The Western Vision of the Ohio Company." *Ohio History* 90 (1981): 5–32.

Dunn, Jacob Piatt, Jr. *Indiana, a Redemption from Slavery*. Revised ed. Boston: Houghton Mifflin Co., 1905.

Eblen, Jack E. *The First and Second United States Empires: Governors and Territorial Government, 1784–1912*. Pittsburgh: University of Pittsburgh Press, 1968.

————. "The Origins of the United States Colonial System: The Ordinance of 1787." *Wisconsin Magazine of History* 51 (1968): 294–314. Reprinted in *The Old Northwest in the American Revolution, an Anthology*, edited by David Curtis Skaggs. Madison: The State Historical Society of Wisconsin, 1977.

Force, Peter. "The Ordinance of 1787 and Its History." In *The St. Clair Papers: The Life and Public Services of Arthur St. Clair*, edited by William Henry Smith. 2 vols. Cincinnati: R. Clarke and Co., 1882.

Galbreath, C.B. "The Ordinance of 1787, Its Origins and Authorship." *Ohio Archaeological and Historical Quarterly* 33 (1924): 110–75.

Gilpin, Alec R. *The Territory of Michigan*. East Lansing: Michigan State University Press, 1970.

Griffin, J. David. "Historians and the Sixth Article of the Ordinance of 1787." *Ohio History* 78 (1969): 252–60.

Haight, Walter C. "The Binding Effect of the Ordinance of 1787." *Publications of the Michigan Political Science Association* 2 (1896–97).

Hawkins, Hubert H., comp. *Indiana's Road to Statehood: A Documentary Record*. Indianapolis: Indiana Historical Bureau, 1969.

Henry, Ruby A. "Background for Kentucky's Constitutional Convention in 1790." *Filson Club Historical Quarterly* 42 (1968): 5–20.

Horsman, Reginald. "American Indian Policy in the Old Northwest, 1783–1812." *William and Mary Quarterly*, 3d ser., 18 (1961): 35–53.

———. *Expansion and American Indian Policy, 1783–1812*. East Lansing: Michigan State University Press, 1967.

———. *The Frontier in the Formative Years, 1783–1815*. New York: Holt, Rinehart, and Winston, Inc., 1970.

Howard, Robert P. *Illinois: A History of the Prairie State*. Grand Rapids: Eerdmans Publishing Co., 1972.

Jensen, Merrill. *The Articles of Confederation: An Interpretation of the Social-Constitutional History of the American Revolution, 1774–1781*. Madison: University of Wisconsin Press, 1959.

———. *The New Nation: A History of the United States during the Confederation, 1781–1789*. New York: Alfred A. Knopf, 1950.

———. "The Cession of the Old Northwest." *Mississippi Valley Historical Review* 23 (1936): 27–48.

———, ed. *The Documentary History of the Ratification of the Constitution*. Vol. 1, *Constitutional Documents and Records, 1776–1787*. Madison: The State Historical Society of Wisconsin, 1976.

Journals of the Continental Congress, 1774–1789. Washington, D.C.: U.S. Government Printing Office, 1904–1937.

Kettleborough, Charles. *Constitution Making in Indiana, A Source Book of Constitutional Documents with Historical Introduction and Critical Notes*. Vol. 1, *1780–1851*. Indiana Historical Collections. Indianapolis: Indiana Historical Bureau, 1916.

Lindley, Harlow; Schneider, Norris F.; and Quaife, Milo M. *His-*

tory of the Ordinance of 1787 and the Old Northwest Territory. Marietta, Ohio: Northwest Territory Celebration Commission, 1937.

Lynd, Staughton. "The Compromise of 1787." *Political Science Quarterly* 81 (1966): 225–50. Reprinted in *The Old Northwest in the American Revolution, an Anthology*, edited by David Curtis Skaggs. Madison: The State Historical Society of Wisconsin, 1977.

Madison, James H. "The Northwest Ordinance and Constitutional Development in Indiana." *International Journal of Social Education* 2 (1987).

Onuf, Peter S. "Towards Federalism: Virginia, Congress, and the Western Lands." *William and Mary Quarterly*, 3d ser., 34 (1977): 353–74.

———. "From Colony to Territory: Changing Concepts of Statehood in Revolutionary America." *Political Science Quarterly* 97 (1982): 447–59.

———. *The Origins of the Federal Republic: Jurisdictional Controversies in the United States, 1775–1787*. Philadelphia: University of Pennsylvania Press, 1983.

———. "From Constitution to Higher Law: The Reinterpretation of the Northwest Ordinance." *Ohio History* 94 (1985): 5–33.

———. "Liberty, Development, and Union: Visions of the West in the 1780s." *William and Mary Quarterly*, 3d ser., 43 (1986): 179–213.

———. *Statehood and the Union: A History of the Northwest Ordinance*. Bloomington: Indiana University Press, 1987.

Owen, Daniel. "Circumvention of Article VI of the Ordinance of 1787." *Indiana Magazine of History* 36 (1940): 110–16.

Patrick, John J. *Lessons on the Northwest Ordinance*. Bloomington, Indiana: The Social Studies Development Center at Indiana University, 1986.

Pease, Theodore C. "The Ordinance of 1787." *Mississippi Valley Historical Review* 25 (1938): 167–80.

Philbrick, Francis F. "Introduction." *The Laws of Indiana Territory, 1801–1809*. Collections of the Illinois State Historical Library. Vol. 21, 1930. Reprint with supplementary Indiana material, Indianapolis: Indiana Historical Bureau, 1931.

Poole, William Frederick. *The Ordinance of 1787, and Dr. Manasseh Cutler as an Agent in its Formation*. Cambridge, Mass.: Welch, Bigelow, and Co., 1876.

―――. *The Ordinance of 1787. A Reply. By William F. Poole*. Ann Arbor, Michigan: privately printed, 1892.

"Publius," [Madison], "The Federalist No. 43 [42]." In *The Federalist*, edited by Jacob E. Cooke. Middletown, Conn.: Wesleyan University Press, [1961]. 288–98.

Quaife, Milo M. "The Significance of the Ordinance of 1787." Illinois State Historical Society, *Journal* 30 (1938): 415–28.

Robinson, Donald. *Slavery in the Structure of American Politics, 1765–1820*. New York, 1971.

Rohrbough, Malcolm J. *The Trans-Appalachian Frontier: People, Societies, and Institutions, 1775–1850*. New York: Oxford University Press, 1978.

Shriver, Phillip R. "America's Other Bicentennial." *The Old Northwest* 9 (1983): 219–35.

Skaggs, David Curtis, ed. *The Old Northwest in the American Revolution, an Anthology*. Madison: The State Historical Society of Wisconsin, 1977.

Smith, William Henry, ed. *The St. Clair Papers: The Life and Public Services of Arthur St. Clair…with His Correspondence and Other Papers*. 2 vols. Cincinnati: R. Clarke and Co., 1882. Reprint, New York: Da Capo Press, 1971.

Smoot, Joseph G. "Freedom's Early Ring: The Northwest Ordinance and the American Union." Ph.D. dissertation, University of Kentucky, 1964.

Stone, Frederick D. "The Ordinance of 1787." *Pennsylvania Magazine of History and Biography* 25 (1938): 167–80.

Strong, Moses M. *History of the Wisconsin Territory, from 1836 to 1848*. Madison: Democratic Printing Co., state printers, 1885.

Swan, William O. "The Northwest Ordinances, So-Called and Confusion." *Historical Education Quarterly* 51 (1965): 235–40.

Wiecek, William M. *The Sources of Antislavery Constitutionalism in America, 1760–1848*. Ithaca: Cornell University Press, 1977.

Index